BAIN
and
BEYOND

Also by Joe Karam:

David and Goliath: The Bain Family Murders (1997)

BAIN
and
BEYOND

Joe Karam

REED

This book is dedicated to Bernadine and Joe,
my mum and dad

Published by Reed Books, a division of Reed Publishing (NZ) Ltd,
39 Rawene Rd, Birkenhead, Auckland.
Associated companies, branches and representatives throughout the world.

Established in 1907, Reed Publishing (NZ) Ltd
is New Zealand's largest book publisher, with over 300 titles in print.

For details on all these books visit our website:
www.reed.co.nz

ISBN 0 7900 0747 9

First published 2000
© Joe Karam 2000
The author asserts his moral rights in the work.

Printed in New Zealand

Contents

Foreword

Unlike the contributors of most forewords, I am not a high-profile person vouching for the character or expertise of a writer. However, when asked to write some words to precede *Bain and Beyond*, I was delighted at the opportunity because the Bain case, and particularly my father's involvement in it, has played a significant part in my life over the last four and a half years. Indeed, to a large extent they have shaped my life.

During that four and a half year period, I have spent a year at school, a year working, and two and a half years at law school in Christchurch, and the Bain case, and Dad, have never been out of the public eye for long. It is in this context that I offer a few perspectives on the issue and the man behind it.

One such perspective is that of someone who is seen as being close to the action, and thus is often questioned about the Bain case. Questions such as: 'Have you met him?' 'Do you think he is innocent?' To which I am able to tell people that I visit David regularly and find him to be a very pleasant and normal bloke.

But the question I have been asked most often, particularly in the early days of Dad's involvement, is 'Why is he doing it?' Most people find the idea of a layperson fighting the whole establishment to prove the innocence of someone they didn't even know before beyond comprehension. Indeed, even I find that concept overwhelming at times.

On reflection, I have realised that one key problem people have with such a 'cause' is that generally no one really does anything about an issue unless their personal experience has made them feel very strongly about it — or, for example, if there are valuable votes to be gained. So when a person takes up a cause in which these factors are not obvious, we are instantly suspicious of his motives. When I am asked this question and tell people Dad's motives I can almost read what some of them are thinking: 'Hang on. Nobody does this. What's the *real* story behind this Joe Karam? What's in it for him? There *must* be an ulterior motive.' Certainly this is the attitude many sections of the media have preferred.

I'm sure it is rather obvious now, but I don't think the extent of Dad's altruistic devotion to David's plight, and particularly the substance behind that devotion, has been given its full recognition at times. Once you are absolutely convinced of someone's innocence, and have uncovered an abundance of evidence that supports your opinion, how could you possibly turn your back on that person and carry on living the good life? This is certainly Dad's rationale and is a personal quality in him that I really admire and respect. This book adds to that abundance of evidence.

The second perspective I offer is that of a young law student who is soon to enter the legal system. At law school the key focus is on teaching students the law and how it is applied. It seems to me that in criminal justice there is an underlying assumption that the police always remain objective throughout an investigation, follow up all possible avenues thoroughly, and then give evidence frankly and openly in the ensuing trial. Unfortunately, this has been found not to be so, and watching official police responses in the defamation case, knowing the opposite to be true, has been a real eye-opener. An example of this is the unrelenting assertion by the police that the Bain investigation was carried out in a 'copybook' manner. This view was endorsed by a combined police/Police Complaints Authority review into

8 ·

the case, and no doubt prompted the defamation proceedings against my father by two of the officers involved in the case, who saw *David and Goliath* as an attack on their 'copybook' policing and honesty.

The defamation case was not only a test of the integrity and thoroughness of the man who called their actions into question, but also a test of the factual accuracy of his entire book. I attended the whole defamation trial, and from a law student's perspective it provided a remarkable insight into the workings of the court system. The conclusions reached by twelve ordinary New Zealanders have served to shatter the 'copybook' myth once and for all, and confirm that the 'allegations' in *David and Goliath* weren't merely a rant by someone trying to sell a few books.

I undoubtedly learned much more about reality from attending this trial than I lost by missing a couple of weeks of lectures. One of the key lessons was that the underlying assumption of police objectivity can be a very dangerous one to make. To personally witness senior police officers from a major homicide inquiry admit that extensive evidence given at the trial was false and contrived, and to see them prevaricate on the stand, rammed this home to me.

Finally, the effect this case has had on our family life over the past few years has been enormous. In the past when people recognised my surname they would comment on Dad's rugby prowess and success. Now people were questioning his motives and integrity, and in many cases were openly critical of him. This was unnerving, particularly given the standing that All Blacks have in this country. These factors have led to a very frustrating and lonely period in Dad's life.

So the last four and a half years have been a real sacrifice. Not just for Dad, but also for Richard, Simone and me. The financial pressure of funding this crusade has been unbelievable, for him and therefore for the three of us. But none of us resents a single cent of it because we could not be more proud of our father and the massive task he has taken on, for the sole purpose of giving an innocent young man his life back.

I'm sure this book will mean as much to you as a New Zealander as it does to me. Here's hoping the next book is *Jail and Beyond*, by David Bain.

Matthew A. Karam
June 2000

Prologue

David Bain — an innocent man?

In May of 1997, the Police Commissioner called for an internal investigation into the allegations in my previous book, *David and Goliath: The Bain Family Murders*. This review became a joint investigation by the Police Complaints Authority (PCA) and the New Zealand Police. Their report was released publicly on 26 November 1997.

The very beginning of the 112-page document lists what it calls 'the points which mainly support the police contention that David Bain rather than his father [Robin] was the killer.'

There are seventeen such points, and I list them as follows, with a response to each one.

1. David's rifle and ammunition were used to commit the murders. The weapon was taken from David's room and the trigger lock undone with a key kept in his room.

   New evidence. *An expert scientific photographer who has given evidence for the Crown on numerous occasions on footprints and shoe prints in carpet, and who was recommended to the PCA by police national headquarters for his expertise, has found imprints of the soles of the shoes Robin Bain was wearing that morning in David's room, in front of the cupboard where the rifle was kept, and in front of the dresser on which the trinket box containing the key was kept. The trigger lock and some ammunition are actually lying on top of one of these prints.*

2. The bloodstained gloves worn by the offender were David's and had been taken from a drawer in his room.

11

New evidence. *The shoe impressions of his father were in front of the drawer. Possible traces of blood were seen by the Institute of Environment Science and Research Limited (ESR) scientist in fingernail scrapings from Robin, but never analysed, and their existence not disclosed to the defence or the court.*

3. David's fingerprints, impressed while wet with blood, were found on the rifle.

   Response. *The fingerprints were in the opposite position to those in which they would have been had David been holding the rifle in a firing position.*

   New evidence. *There is no evidence that the blood in which the fingerprints were made is human. There is compelling new DNA evidence that the blood was that of an animal, and not human. (See additional detail, chapter 7.)*

4. Significantly, his father's fingerprints were not on the rifle.

   New evidence. *Data from US and Australian experts proves that it is very rare for the fingerprints of the perpetrator of a homicide — murder or suicide — to be found on the firearm used. It is only in about two per cent of cases that such fingerprints are found. This was not known to the jury at the trial.*

5. David had a bloodstain on his shorts which was either Stephen's, Arawa's or Laniet's, and two droplets of blood on his socks. There was other bloodstaining on his socks, and there were clear impressions of 280-mm long stockinged feet made in blood on carpet which were visible by luminol testing.

   Response. *The 'stain' on his shorts was so minute as to be undetectable by the naked eye. The drops on his socks were on the underside; they were white socks, and there was no blood on the* upper surfaces, as would have been the case if he had been in a bloody struggle with Stephen as alleged by the Crown.

New evidence. *The footprints were said by the police to be 280-mm long. David's feet are 300-mm long, so they could not be his. His father's, without socks, were measured during the post-mortem at 275 mm. The jury was not told either of those facts — only that Robin's socks were 240 mm. The Court was told that photos of these footprints did not come out; David's lawyer was led to believe they were under- or over-exposed. This was untrue — the photos did come out but do not show any footprints or anything remotely resembling a footprint. There was no blood inside the shoes David had worn that morning. David had been into various rooms in the house. Such blood as there was on his clothes is consistent with brushing against bloodstained surfaces, and walking on a bloodstained floor, but quite inconsistent with what would be expected to be on his clothes if he had shot five people at point-blank range, and been involved in a bloody struggle as alleged.*

6. A lens from the damaged spectacles located in David's room was found in Stephen's room . . . It was presumed he was wearing an old pair kept in the house and that in the course of the struggle with Stephen the left lens was sprung from the frame and fell on the floor.

Response. *At the trial and subsequently it was alleged that the glasses were an old pair of David's, even though that was known to be untrue. The lens was said in evidence to be visible on the floor, as shown on a photograph, where it could have fallen. That evidence is now known and admitted to be untrue by the detective who gave it. The lens was in fact under a boot which was in turn under folded clothing where it could not possibly have fallen. Moreover, there is no evidence that David wore those glasses that* *weekend, and there is evidence that he was not wearing any glasses that weekend. There was no blood, hair or fingerprints on the lens to link it to the events of that day.*

7. David bore recent signs of injury consistent with a struggle with Stephen before he was killed. A small piece of skin which could have come from a recent knee injury of David's was found in Stephen's room. There were recent bruises to his face and an abrasion above his right eye which probably occurred when the spectacles were damaged.

   Response. *The police pathologist had physically compared the piece of skin in question with Stephen's hand injury and concluded that it had probably come from that injury. The police did not disclose this information to David's defence lawyer, but instead continued to produce evidence at the trial to show it came from David's knee, knowing that to be contrary to the pathologist's conclusion. The abrasion was above the right eye, whereas the left lens was alleged to have been dislodged in the struggle. Such minor injuries as David had were consistent with those he would have sustained blundering around the darkened untidy house in a state of shock. He also collapsed that morning in the presence of the police, banging his head against the wall.*

8. Significantly, Robin Bain did not show similar signs of recent involvement in a struggle. Minor semi-healed nicks on his hands were considered unrelated.

   New evidence. *There is now a substantial body of expert opinion from pathologists of great experience and reputation in Australia to exactly the opposite effect.*

9. The position of the cartridge case in the computer alcove was consistent with the barrel of the rifle being poked through the gap in the curtains from inside the alcove when it was

fired, which together with the position of the wound, rifle and body is inconsistent with Robin shooting himself.

New evidence. *Expert comparison of photographs since the trial proves there was significant contamination of the scene even after it was supposedly secured. This heightens the likelihood of even more significant contamination by accidental movement of objects, especially cartridge cases lying on the floor, as the first police and ambulance personnel moved through the house. In any event the police case that Robin could not have shot himself is now debunked by independent experts from overseas. Additionally, the original pathologist's notes, not disclosed to the defence, show that he himself concluded it was 'perfectly feasible' for someone of his build (similar to Robin Bain's) to have reached the trigger and shot himself.*

10. When David spoke to the 111 operator he said 'they are all dead', which is inconsistent with what he said later to a police officer to the effect he had seen only the bodies of his mother and father.

    New evidence. *Evidence from an eminent forensic psychiatrist who examined David before the trial and has counselled him weekly for the last five years, not called at the trial, is that David suffered acute stress reaction from discovering the horrific scene within the house, and has continued to suffer from post-traumatic stress disorder. His disjointed memory, confusion and memory gaps are symptoms of these disorders and such inconsistencies are to be expected.*

11. David's bloodied palm-print was found on the washing machine in which bloodstained garments had apparently been washed.

    Response. *There is no evidence that 'bloodstained garments' had* *been washed. This is speculation. Close examination of the evidence shows that the palm-print alleged to have been made in blood was not red in colour, and was only visible after various processes were used which give reactions to substances other than blood. David usually did the washing. It is not surprising his palm-print was on the machine.*

12. David could not adequately account for his actions in the period of around 25 minutes between his return home after the paper round and dialling 111.

    Response. *See response to point 10. Did they really expect him to be unemotional and totally lucid and clear? If he were and was as devious and cunning as they claim, is it really likely he would have made such an obvious blunder?*

13. A target found in David's room comprised five circles which could represent five heads. All five family members had head wounds.

    Response. *This goes beyond metaphysics into the realm of voodoo and witchcraft. Do the police expect anyone to take such unmitigated nonsense seriously? It simply shows how bankrupt their 'reasoning' is.*

14. The presence of a blood spot in the porcelain basin in the laundry was not consistent with David having washed his hands to remove printer's ink after the paper round.

    Response. *Another non sequitur. With six people using a hand basin, spots of blood are common from activities like cleaning teeth or shaving. Look at your own hand basin after the kids have used it. How does this 'inconsistency' sit with the absence of blood on David's hands when he was supposed to have handled the rifle with bloody hands?*

15. The use of the expression 'deserved to stay' rather than 'deserved to live' has a link with David collapsing and saying that he saw 'black hands coming to take him away' and the use of the past tense of 'deserve' indicates it was not Robin who wrote that message on the computer.

    Response. *More metaphysics and voodoo, without a scrap of supporting evidence from an expert linguist. A linguist consulted subsequently has dismissed this as utter nonsense.*

16. In his evidence at trial, David said he could now recall things he could not at the time he was interviewed by the police. For example, at first he could not remember going into the bedroom of his sisters and brother, but now remembered going into all rooms and actually touching his brother.

    New evidence. *The opinion of the expert forensic psychiatrist referred to is that this is perfectly normal for someone who has suffered a severely traumatising experience and has acute stress reaction followed by post-traumatic stress disorder. Also, his 'memory' may not be a true memory, but may have been implanted by reading and hearing the evidence at the depositions and trial. Eleven months elapsed between the murders and the trial, during which false memories could have been implanted.*

17. David gave evidence at the trial that he heard Laniet gurgling. The Crown said that because only the third shot to Laniet was fatal, only the killer could have heard her gurgling, because she could not have made such sounds after death.

    New evidence. *Expert pathological evidence from overseas has shown this allegation to be untrue, because the Crown theory of the sequence of shots to Laniet is demonstrably wrong, and there is evidence from people with experience of this phenomenon that* *the accumulated blood and gas in her lungs could produce gurgling sounds even after death. The ESR scientific evidence was hopelessly astray on this matter. Cotton fibres on the bullet fragments which I could see with the naked eye were not even noticed by the ballistics 'expert' from the ESR.*

Significantly, this list includes all of the twelve main points of evidence put to the jury by the Crown and discussed by the judge in his summing up to the jury at David's trial — except for one critical factor. I cannot help but reflect that the omission of this point is tacit acknowledgement by the police that the evidence given at the trial in this regard was wrong.

This point was that the message on the computer could only have been put there by the killer. The Crown theory at trial was that the computer was turned on after David got home from doing his paper round, and that he turned it on and wrote the message when he got home, as part of a premeditated plan to implicate his father.

Response. *The time at which the computer was turned on was determined by a computer expert. He relied upon a detective recording the time of various functions. The detective used his own watch to record these timings. His watch was later found to be two minutes fast. In addition, the analysis of the computer expert was astray by 57 seconds. These two factors, when put into the calculation, mean that the computer was actually switched on three minutes earlier than originally calculated.*

This means that David was not home when it was switched on. Despite knowing this, the police did not tell the jury, and defence counsel failed to pick up this point of crucial importance. (For a detailed analysis see chapter 7.)

In light of these factors, then, I invite a consideration of the following analysis:

a. There was a message on the computer, 'Sorry you are the only one who deserved to stay.' Unquestionably, and undisputed by the Crown, the killer turned on the computer and wrote this message.

b. The only time that can be identified with absolute precision in this case is the minute that the computer was turned on. This time was put to the court in David Bain's trial inaccurately as 6.44 a.m. It was actually 6.41 a.m.

c. It is beyond any argument that at that time David Bain was still doing his paper round. David Bain could therefore not have been the writer of this message.

d. The evidence (points 3, 6, 8, 11, 12, 13, 15, 17 above) that the police attribute to David as the killer, can more logically be attributed to David as the 'finder' of his dead family.

e. No evidence of motive or mental disorder has ever been attributed to David Bain.

f. However, there is substantial evidence that Robin was in a state of severe mental deterioration at the time of the tragedies. There is also substantial evidence that a 'trigger' or precipitating factor existed for Robin that very weekend, in the form of Laniet's express intention to expose the alleged incestuous relationship between herself and her father.

g. Robin Bain's death carries all the hallmarks of suicide — a contact wound to the temple and rifle lying beside the body. This statement is corroborated by two eminent Australian pathologists, and is by the original pathologist's post-mortem notes which were not disclosed to the defence or the jury.

Conclusion

If David Bain were to be tried tomorrow before any jury in the world, on the facts as they are now known, it would acquit him as resoundingly as did the jury who heard the evidence in the recent defamation proceedings against me.

David Bain is innocent!

Introduction

On 9 June 2000, just eleven days ago as I write, Justice Noel Anderson completed his summing up to the jury in the High Court in Auckland. This was the penultimate act in the two-week High Court trial in which two members of the Bain police inquiry team charged me with having defamed them in my book *David and Goliath*, which had been published some three years earlier. The plaintiffs were (former) Detective Sergeant Milton Weir and Detective Sergeant Kevin Anderson. (Weir 'perfed' from the police in 1999, and Anderson was promoted from detective to detective sergeant at the time of the police/PCA review.)

For me, sitting at the back of the court with my family and friends, it was as though World War III was about to come to an abrupt end, yet as I faced that realisation I was also acutely aware that this was really only another battle on the way to winning the actual war.

As I listened to the judge, I realised that I was sapped of every last ounce of mental and emotional energy. I had been running on adrenalin, I suppose, for the past few months and now, as His Honour delivered his final few words, I realised there was no more I could do. I was also all too aware of the effect the outcome would have on the war in which I had become embroiled with the New Zealand Police, and the New Zealand criminal justice system.

The trial had begun on Friday, 26 May with a pre-trial hearing, in which the two sides argued various aspects of the case before the judge. We lost a major battle that day, when the judge allowed a late amendment to the plaintiffs' major claim, but while I found this particularly disturbing, it also served to deepen my resolve and that of my barrister, Julian Miles QC.

The war had begun some four years ago, when on 19 June 1996 I had visited the regional commander of police in Dunedin to amicably discuss my concerns regarding the safety of the conviction of David Bain for the murders of his family. This was my first contact with the police. Their response set in train a course of events that ultimately led to the trial which has consumed me for the past few months.

The police response was delivered to me a couple of days later by Michael Guest, at the time David Bain's lawyer. He advised me that the Dunedin CIB had phoned his office to say that all exhibits relating to David's conviction were to be destroyed! I was shocked and disturbed — what did they have to hide?

Guest wrote to the police expressing his dismay and protesting vehemently at this course of action. I faxed a letter of protest to a variety of people including the Minister of Police, the commissioner of police, the Minister of Justice, the regional commander of police in Dunedin, and the Ombudsman. As far as I know nothing was destroyed.

And so the battle lines were drawn. Clearly, I was not likely to receive any assistance from the police in regard to my concerns! Be that as it may, I still tried to resolve the problem by visiting the Commissioner of Police, Peter Doone, in Wellington in October 1996. That meeting also proved futile, and so later that year I began to write *David and Goliath*, which was published on 16 April 1997.

The police took extreme exception to the contents of the book, and set up an internal inquiry to examine what they called the 'unfounded allegations' it contained. This inquiry, which became a joint effort between the police and the PCA, began almost immediately after the book's publication. The report of the inquiry was released on 26 November 1997, about six months later, in a blaze of publicity. It found that the police inquiry into the Bain case was an exemplary effort, and it cleared all officers involved in the case of any wrongdoing. Ominously, when releasing the report Commissioner Doone made reference to the possibility that some officers may feel inclined to institute legal proceedings against me.

In April 1998 I was served with papers indicating that Milton Weir and Kevin Anderson were suing me for defamation, claiming both compensatory and punitive damages amounting to about $500,000.

And so here we were, two years later, in the High Court; all that was left was for the jury to reach and announce its verdict.

My children had gathered in support of me. My eldest son Richard, who lives in Auckland, took as much time off work to attend the court as he could manage, along with his girlfriend Kelly. Matthew, a third-year law student in Christchurch, came up and attended almost the entire trial. Simone, my seventeen-year-old daughter, was also with me throughout. My children's support and encouragement has been selfless and committed throughout, and never more apparent than during the two weeks of the trial. Dinah, my girlfriend, accepted me as I was — highly strung, totally preoccupied, single-minded to the point of being difficult and unpleasant company for much of the time — and never once did she flinch. I shall never forget her support.

Others turned up to lend their support. Arthur Allan Thomas's brother Ray came in one day; he knows what it is to fight the police. Old friends attended, as did a number of David's supporters. One of the staunchest of these, Leila Read, came all the way up from Waikanae and sat through the final week. Two television channels had their cameras set up in the court, and of course other media representatives were in attendance.

The judge finished his summing up to the jury at 12.45 p.m., with words to the effect that the book *David and Goliath* was the cornerstone of the case for both sides. Did the book carry the meaning that the plaintiffs claimed? he asked the jury, and if it did, did it support those meanings with facts that *were proven to be true and correct*? It was a complex case, he said, and these were matters for you, and you alone, he told them.

We left the court to have some lunch. I had a minor altercation with Julian Miles, my QC. Nerves were frayed, and I lost my cool. I shouldn't have, and I regret it, but Julian handled me with dignified aplomb and I thank him for that. Alan Smith, the managing director of Reed Publishing (NZ) Ltd, my publishers, tried to calm me down, and I let him have a bit of a salvo too. He also showed understanding. A couple of the judge's rulings had upset me (unnecessarily as it turned out), but deep down I knew that whatever the outcome Julian had been a magnificent advocate, both professionally and in the manner that his belief in me was communicated to the court.

As the day wore on my loyal band stayed with me. Nerves became even more frayed, more coffee was consumed, we ran out of smokes as we paced the foyer of the High Court building. Strangely, as everyone else became more and more on edge, by about 5 p.m. a peaceful calm began to come over me. My old schoolmate and First Fifteen team-mate, Colin, called in and said, 'You've nothing to worry about, mate. You were supremely sure of your facts when giving evidence, in stark contrast to the other side, and the jury will see that.'

I wasn't so sure, but by this time I felt pretty good. A quick verdict, it was thought, would be in our favour. The longer it went on the more likely that a compromise verdict or worse still, a ruling against me, may result. The judge had presented the jury with a list of nineteen issues on which they had to decide, which included the amount of the damages if they found against me. If this was the case, it would significantly add to the time.

At about 5.30 I looked at the list of issues and wrote down what I thought the jury would find. As it turned out I was absolutely correct with respect to the major claimant, Milton Weir, and only slightly astray in respect of Anderson.

By six o'clock the tension was becoming almost tangible. It was heightened by news that the jury did not intend to take their dinner break at 6.30. The verdict must be imminent.

Soon after 8 p.m. we were notified that the jury was ready to deliver. We filed back into court, tired and stressed. The cameras were rolling, the press had pens expectantly in hand, the photographers were lined up outside the court, cameras loaded.

Dinah and Matthew said to me, 'It's amazing, you seem to be the calmest of us all.' I answered that the battle had been fought, there was no more we could do. But deep inside I was all too aware of the ramifications for David Bain, and for Joe Karam and Colin Withnall as his advocates, of the news we were about to get. I was also aware of the ramifications for the New Zealand Police, but I knew that they had launched this case in the expectation that it would deliver the knock-out punch to Joe Karam once and for all.

The jury filed in. There was no indication in their demeanour of which way they had gone. Weir and Anderson looked to me much more ill at ease than I felt.

The foreman rose to his feet and began to answer the nineteen issues put before the jury, on the five remaining claims against me.

Claim one, a win for Joe.

Claim two, an even bigger win for me, exactly as I had predicted at 5.30. 'That's Weir done with,' I thought. Now to Anderson, claims three, four and five. Win, win and win again.

My God, a clean sweep. A complete vindication. Even more emphatic than I had expected.

An enormous feeling of satisfaction welled up inside me, and I was reminded of a comment I had made on the *Holmes* programme some four years earlier: 'The truth has its own strange way of revealing itself.' In this case, it had surfaced because *'they'* sued *me*.

It had been a long and arduous battle that had tested my fortitude more than once, but right then it all seemed worth it. The judge pronounced judgement, which was accepted by counsel for both parties, then thanked the jury and left the courtroom.

The realisation set in for everyone in the room as we began to file out of the court. Cameras were flashing, television cameras rolling. We hugged and kissed. Tears of joy and relief were shed, but I had to speak to the media.

'This win is for David,' I said triumphantly, according to the newspapers the following morning.

Julian Miles invited us all to the Northern Club. He ordered champagne.

My phone rang, a thousand times it seemed. The mood was euphoric. Speeches were made, cigars lit, and as the impact of the result began to set in we reminisced about the past few weeks.

I spoke to Colin Withnall QC, my great ally throughout this battle. 'Whoopee,' he yelled into the phone from Dunedin. 'When are you coming down? I've got a bottle of something special in the fridge I've been saving for this day!' Good on you,

Colin, we would not have made it without you.

We partied into the night at the Viaduct Basin, and after a couple of hours' sleep, and with an extremely sore head, I awoke the next day to a weekend of phone calls and press interviews. It took me about a week to recover from the turmoil that has been my own 'four-year war' and settle back into the business of securing justice for David Bain, which will surely now be forthcoming.

It has just occurred to me, as I write these words, that it is the sixth anniversary of the deaths of the Bain family.

Part I
Bain

Chapter 1
Preamble

This book spans four years of my life; four very tumultuous years. It is partly about me, the person, and the emotional and other pressures that I have endured. It also describes many of the incidents, personalities and experiences to which I have been exposed by my involvement with the criminal justice system.

Naturally I could not have undergone these experiences without forming opinions and developing ideas on the workings of our justice system. What began four years ago as an altruistic effort to help a person in desperate need has turned into a conflict that has raised far greater issues than simply one man's innocence.

I am not a lawyer, nor am I a journalist, nor am I an academic, so I do not write as an academic, a journalist, or a legalist. I write as a citizen of a country of which I am very proud, and so really I write on behalf of all the citizens of this country.

One of the side effects that has occurred as a result of my endeavours has been the intense public debate surrounding the case. Looking back, I could probably have done with the assistance of a public relations firm to help me handle all the media and public attention.

One of the most consistent followers of events has been the *Holmes* show, which is, apart from the television news, the most popular current affairs programme in New Zealand. I have been a fairly frequent occupier of an often hot seat on the programme, and as a result I have been invited to the last four *Holmes* Christmas parties. These take the form of an hour-long on-air extravaganza, which broadly canvasses the people and issues the programme has dealt with in the preceding year.

Love him or hate him, Paul Holmes is, apart from being a cheeky fellow and a clever fellow, a very human fellow. He is at his best with human interest stories, and has a genuine capacity to develop an empathy with people of all types and circumstances. And so the guest list at a *Holmes* Christmas party is a cross-section of people one is unlikely to find under any one roof anywhere else. Jammed in like sardines, usually on a humid and sweaty Auckland evening, are All Black captains and their subordinates; current and former prime ministers; senior partners from law firms, come down from their ivory towers; Maori activists, some of them tattooed horrifyingly; disabled couples and the intellectually handicapped; victims of floods and other disasters; even, on one occasion, Jake the dog, who didn't actually get a bark in, as it happened.

A seething mass of disparate humanity, among whom the little tyrant capers, asking questions that are sometimes cheeky, sometimes imploring, and sometimes a bit trite, but almost without fail getting a laugh and touching a soft spot.

Needless to say, one meets people one would not normally come across, and there are some interesting interactions. At the first party I attended, in 1996, David Lange was puddling around, looking a bit disdainful, and appearing rather lonely. He seemed to disappear quite early. Before he did I attempted to make myself known to him, but he just turned his back on me. I was a little surprised, slightly miffed, and naturally curious. The answer, perhaps, came along six months later, when James McNeish's book *Mask of Sanity* was published, complete with a commendation from David Lange! Perhaps Lange's stance on the secret service at recent select committee hearings (where he strongly supported their right to break into our homes) provides the clue to this unlikely partnership, bearing in mind that McNeish's book was written with the assistance of the New Zealand Police! Then again, perhaps it is simply that the big ex-lawyer from Otahuhu is another in the profession who finds it distasteful that an ordinary New Zealand citizen should be concerned about common justice. Justice should be left to the professionals, and all that.

At the *Holmes* Christmas shindig the following year, the most interesting encounters I had were with Arthur Allan Thomas and his wife, and Sir Robert Jones. I had quite a chat with Thomas, and I was impressed with the attitude he has brought to his life subsequent to his release from prison in 1979. Touching on the so-called family feud — which has since been blown out of all proportion in the media — he expressed in his simple way the undoubtedly well-founded truism that 'where there's money, there's problems', in reference to his million-dollar compensation payment.

Sir Robert and I have since developed quite a friendship. Unlike others who say they admire Bob despite his outspokenness, I can honestly say that I like him because of it. Anyone who has managed to engage in half the shenanigans he has, while amassing, retaining and expanding a fortune at the same time, is in my opinion entitled to speak his own mind. Sir Robert does not suffer fools, women drivers or traffic police gladly, but who are we to say he is wrong?

Not long after I had arrived at the 1998 Christmas party, I looked up to see the Commissioner of Police, Peter Doone, walk in. He was in civvies — an open-necked shirt, the sort of dress you would wear to a barbecue — in striking contrast to the police regalia we normally see commissioners in. To my astonishment he made a beeline for me, smiling like a Cheshire cat, and put his hand out to shake hands as if we were long-lost buddies. I had of course had a number of dealings with him at police headquarters in Wellington, and we had appeared together many times on various television shows. I looked at him quizzically, wondering if this was some kind of prank set up for the cameras, but it wasn't.

He said something like: 'Oh well, Joe, it's the season of goodwill and I thought it would be nice to have a pleasant chat with you.' I was dumbfounded, and replied along the lines of: 'It's a shame your spirit of goodwill only comes out at Christmas when you're off duty.'

A few awkward comments followed before he melted away into the crowd. As history records, Doone's meltdown is now complete.

I was again invited to the *Holmes* Christmas party in 1999, but I had decided at the time of submitting the petition for David Bain's pardon to the Governor-General that I would resist the temptation to be inveigled into media speculation about proceedings. So I decided not to attend that year. (I had not expected then, that eighteen months later the petition would still be being processed.)

Maybe the *Holmes* Christmas party of 2000 will be a celebratory one, which I will attend accompanied by a special guest — one who has been restricted to watching the previous parties from behind bars!

Chapter 2

David and Goliath
— the lead-up

The period of my life immediately following the publication of *David and Goliath* on 16 April 1997, through to the submission of our petition to the Governor-General in June 1998, was characterised by a whirlwind of drama. *David and Goliath* was an outstanding success in terms of its sales and readership. The initial print run of 10,000 sold out within days, as did the second run of 10,000. Had more books been printed initially sales would have been even greater, as many people were unable to get copies during the first week when the publicity surrounding it was at its most intense. Be that as it may, it sold over 30,000 copies, a stupendous number in a market the size of New Zealand. I received many calls from people who had attempted to get a copy of the book from their local library, only to find that the reserve list could have up to twenty or thirty names on it.

So what was *David and Goliath* all about, and what led to its publication?

My involvement with the Bain case began in January 1996. One Monday morning I read an article in the *New Zealand Herald* describing how some of David Bain's friends intended to form a committee and start a campaign to raise funds to fight to prove his innocence. They were a disparate group of mostly young people, friends of David's from university and the Opera Live

Society, as well as an elderly lady who had been his singing teacher. I was struck by the nature of this group, as it seemed they could have no motive apart from an intense belief in David's innocence.

Until then the Bain case had not been of particular interest to me. At the time of the Bain family's deaths in June 1994 I owned a fast-growing business which had branches on both sides of the Tasman. I was a busy man, travelling New Zealand and Australia on quite a rigorous schedule. In addition, my marriage of some twenty years was in a bad way; although my wife and I had reconciled at the time I read the *Herald* article in January 1996, the marriage was to end soon afterwards.

Anyway, I was quite struck by this article, and discussed it with my wife, Robin, to see whether she knew any more about the case. The situation at that time was that David had been convicted in June 1995 of killing his entire family, and his conviction had been sustained in December 1995 by the Court of Appeal. Hence the group forming to begin a new fight in January 1996.

My wife recalled having read some articles and following the story on the news, and was particularly struck by what she described as the 'strangeness of the case against David and the rather bizarre burning down of the Bain family home just days after David had been arrested'.

For some reason — David and his supporters would say some God-sent reason — I could not get the case out of my mind. I found out that David's lawyer had been Michael Guest, and made contact with him. My initial intention was simply to make a donation to the group, if in fact it seemed a worthwhile cause. Well, as *David and Goliath* records, and this book will further demonstrate, it was not only a worthwhile cause, it was a cause that would come to completely dominate my life for over four years.

I met Michael Guest soon after making contact with him, and also had some meetings with David in Christchurch's Paparua prison. It quickly became apparent that there were significant gaps in the evidence on which David was convicted, and that Guest himself had become quite consumed by the fact that David had suffered a miscarriage of justice.

Soon, through an arrangement with Guest whereby I funded his costs to seek leave to appeal to the Privy Council, he appointed me a member of the 'Bain defence team'. This gave me official access to his entire file, and also the capacity to visit David at any time. Since then I have come to know David very well indeed, having visited him maybe sixty or so times, as well as maintaining constant contact by phone and post.

I completed an initial study of the records supplied to me by Guest during February and March 1996. These included all his internal memos relating to the case, the complete file released to him by the New Zealand Police — all witness statements and interviews, job sheets, forensic analysis reports and the like, the entire trial transcript and two booklets of photos and a video used as exhibits at the trial. This study revealed to me many anomalies and contradictions in the case put to the jury in David Bain's trial.

The Privy Council appeal was heard on 29 April 1996 and, predictably, it was unsuccessful. At this time my association with the case became public for the first time when I was filmed by TV One leaving the Privy Council hearing in London.

I came back to New Zealand with a momentous decision to make. How far would I go? How far *could* I go? By what means could I advance the situation, even if sufficient evidence could be gathered? Even with all the thought I put into this decision at the time, I could never have imagined just how momentous it would turn out to be.

Of course at the time I was politically, and certainly legally, extremely naive. I am not a lawyer, I have had no legal training, and until I became involved in this case I had never been any closer to a court of law than watching *Perry Mason* and *Rumpole of the Bailey* on television (apart from the mandatory couple of traffic offences sustained over the years).

As it has turned out, that naivety has been my greatest strength over the past four years, although it has also exposed me to a lot of consternation, anguish and heartache as well.

I genuinely believed that once the authorities were aware of the unsafeness of David's convictions, then they would be just as concerned as I was. By the authorities, I mean the hierarchy of the New Zealand Police, the Minister of Justice, members of the justice ministry and so on. How wrong I was!

After the Privy Council hearing Michael Guest made it clear that there was no more he could do. I had to make this decision on my own. I spent weeks taking advice and contemplating the problem. I visited David again, many times. On one occasion I was with him for some five hours of the most intense emotional interrogation and discussion imaginable.

I decided I could not let the matter rest. I decided this young man needed and deserved a better deal. I became his last line of defence.

I also decided that my first course of action would be to visit the Dunedin police. Does that convince you of my naivety? I made an appointment with the regional commander in Dunedin, who received me extremely cordially. Athol Soper had been only briefly exposed to the Bain case when he visited the house on the first morning of the tragedy. He assured me of whatever cooperation he could arrange, and during our discussion he made one telling comment. He said that David's arrest caused 'a considerable degree of polarisation amongst members of the Dunedin police at the time'. Athol Soper, though, is in the uniformed, as opposed to the plainclothes, division of the police!

Anyway, he put my concerns before the legal division of the police. I was surprised to get a reply some weeks later, completely refusing any cooperation between myself and the police. The case was closed, they effectively said.

Then a more telling and influential circumstance arose. Within days of my seeing Soper, Michael Guest's office took a phone call from the Dunedin CIB. The message was that the Bain case was now over, exhibits and documents were taking up valuable room, and they intended to dispose of everything at the tip!

Guest immediately notified me. The spectre of the bullet shell disposed of in the tip in the Arthur Allan Thomas case hit me smack in the face. I immediately faxed a letter of protest to a number of officials, including the commissioner of police, the Minister of Justice and the Ombudsman. Nothing was disposed of, but I had now put my finger in the water and caused more than a little ripple.

Well, the rest of 1996 was a bit of a cauldron in itself. I replaced Michael Guest as David's counsel. By this time I had complete power of attorney for David. I appointed O'Driscoll & Marks as his solicitors, and had them instruct Colin Withnall QC as his counsel. I remained officially a member of his defence team. I constructed a considerable brief for Withnall, listing my concerns regarding the case. He agreed to a preliminary examination of these concerns so that he could provide me with advice as to whether he agreed with me, and on a future course of action. I also visited police headquarters in Wellington, where I met the commissioner and assistant commissioner. It was very obvious that the interests of the New Zealand Police did not include David Bain, be he innocent or not.

During David Bain's trial, evidence from Dean Cottle that Robin Bain (David's father) had been involved in an incestuous relationship with his daughter had been disallowed, and Cottle's name and evidence suppressed. Now, however, the *Holmes* programme successfully won an appeal to have the suppression order on Cottle's name and statement lifted. For the first time, vital evidence that Guest had not been able to present fell into the public domain. *Holmes* did two or three programmes on the Bain case with me as the prime focus, and TV3's *20/20* did an hour-long documentary on my involvement. The case of David Bain was very much in the public eye.

By December 1996 Colin Withnall had completed his assessment of my concerns about the case. His conclusions were twofold. Yes, there were serious anomalies in the Crown case against David, so serious that in his opinion David had suffered a miscarriage of justice. And second, the fighting stance taken by the police meant that progress would be hard-fought, tedious and slow. Our avenue for redress would be to seek a royal pardon through the Governor-General under section 406 of the Crimes Act. This petition became our focus.

As I left Colin's office, after what would be our final meeting of 1996, I asked him, 'What can we do to advance this, Colin? I've been on it full time for a year now, and yet despite having achieved a public perception that something is badly wrong, and having identified the various avenues we need to work on, we're really no further ahead. What can we do?'

Sagely, and a little coyly, perhaps, he replied, 'Why don't you write a book about it?'

On the flight home from Dunedin to Auckland I decided to do just that. I had been involved in the case for about a year. I knew the case, and more particularly, the holes in the case off by heart. I had in my possession all the source documents that had been available to the original defence team. Over Christmas I began writing. On 16 April 1997 *David and Goliath: the Bain family murders* was launched amid a blaze of publicity before an audience of 700 people in the Dunedin Town Hall, and transmitted live on the *Holmes* show nationwide.

Chapter 3

The fall-out

On the afternoon of the book launch I met with Steve O'Driscoll and Colin Withnall. Naturally I was pretty nervous. I was well aware of the controversy that my book would provoke, and realised that it would be subjected to extremely intense scrutiny by all sections of the media.

O'Driscoll warned me about alleging police corruption. 'That's the sensational angle, Joe,' he said. 'They're bound to hit you with it. Be very careful. Mistakes, blunders, bungling, omissions — okay. But beware the word "corruption".'

It all seemed pretty much like the same thing to me, but I understood his thrust, and took his advice on board.

Before long, under a blaze of lights, I am live on *Holmes*. Paul, in the Auckland studio, welcomes me and fires the first question at me.

'Joe, your book alleges police corruption in the Bain case.'

'Hang on a minute, Paul,' I interrupt. 'It alleges the police bungled the inquiry, made a premature arrest, and many other mistakes, but it does not allege corruption.'

Thank you, Steve, I thought. Had it not been for his timely warning, I would have surely stumbled in my response to that first question, and landed in even more hot water than I did.

Even so, the tone was set. The battle was in the public domain in no uncertain terms. The police were interviewed and maintained that there was a 'mountain of evidence' against

David, and that they were entirely comfortable with their position.

But in Wellington, the police's legal advisors were working overtime. *David and Goliath* was being dissected word by word. No doubt they were staggered. Never before had such a determined, reasoned and sustained exposé been made of police procedures, police culture and police investigation methods. They knew only one way to deal with it: close ranks and fight back. And that is just what they proceeded to do.

The morning after the launch I conducted nineteen separate interviews with the media, before breakfast! The same theme arose every time: 'How is it that you can be so sure of his innocence when you are just a layperson, in the face of a High Court jury trial, a Court of Appeal hearing, a Privy Council hearing, and experienced senior police officers?'

'Quite simple,' I kept trying to explain. 'The jury simply did not hear all of the evidence, and much of what they did hear was either patently wrong or seriously misleading.'

And I would then proceed to try to give examples. But the detail required to explain a piece of evidence was not what the media were after. They wanted juicy, sexy headlines, not detailed analysis. They tried to put words in my mouth. They attacked me from every angle — my motives; my emotional involvement; my capacity to argue the case at all, not being a member of the legal profession.

I was also attacked by Michael Guest, who was upset by the book, which questioned his efficacy as David's defence lawyer.

Of course, the very approach that I had taken in the book — to pull no punches, tell it exactly as I saw it — in itself demanded this type of reaction. The newspapers invariably allocated one of their crime reporters to reviewing the book and interviewing me.

In many cases these same reporters had covered the Bain trial in the first place. They had trotted out the evidence, accepting it on face value — as they were entitled to, to some extent — and they did not want to backtrack now. The suggestion that the system on which they reported daily could be so patently flawed was simply unpalatable to them. And so, many of the basic premises of the book were misrepresented entirely.

And, of course, they went to the police for their comments, and printed them without any examination. The police line generally reiterated the old story that there was a mountain of evidence against David, followed by a list of this so-called evidence — despite the fact that the book had demonstrated that much of the evidence was seriously, if not totally, flawed.

It would not be unreasonable to say that in most of the interviews I gave, be they on the radio, television or in the press, I was treated in a semi-hostile and sceptical manner. This was particularly the case in the traditional, well-established media, such as the *New Zealand Herald*, the *Dominion*, Christchurch's *Press* and the *Otago Daily Times*, and on National Radio and the ZB stations of Christchurch and Dunedin.

This of course had the effect of undermining the credibility of what I had to say, as it appeared that only the fringe media, so to speak, were printing my point of view.

The week the book was launched, the Bain case, or more pertinently my perspective on the Bain case, was debated on the television news and *Holmes* every night. Over the next few months, newspaper headlines all over the country signalled a stand-off between the police and me: 'Murder inquiry head unmoved', 'Criticism in Karam book unfair', 'Karam reveals blood clue in Bain case', 'Evidence misleading — police sloppy in Bain case — Karam says', 'Ex-cop joins Karam crusade', 'Bain defence told to pursue proper channels', 'Police investigation to review Bain case', 'Police chief — no bias on Bain', 'Police forced to rethink', 'Police may sue over Bain book', 'Karam is sceptical of review', 'Rough justice from flawed system', 'Investigation ill-considered', 'Most MPs back review of Bain inquiry'.

And so it went on. But amid this cacophony of public debate, the work still had to go on. I was really fighting on three separate fronts. The first, which was my primary concern, was to continue to build up the evidence needed to submit an application to the Governor-General for a pardon for David. The second was the public battle being waged between the police and me in the media. And the third was the personal battle to maintain credibility in the public eye, to try to keep my eye on the ball amid the whirlpool of intense scrutiny I was under, and to handle the ever-increasing demands on my time.

However, although I did not expect quite the public furore that followed the publication of *David and Goliath*, it actually meant that the book achieved its aim beyond our wildest dreams. A point that has never been discussed before is that *David and Goliath* was a deliberately provocative book. It was written to raise questions and expose the police to public accountability, so that we could obtain the information we needed to submit the application for David's pardon. It was received as a definitive work, but it was never intended as such.

The fact is that at the time I wrote the book, we had uncovered a raft of unexplainable anomalies in the Crown's case. These included such things as extremely contradictory scientific evidence, pathology evidence that did not make sense, ballistics evidence that did not add up, significant evidence that was never put before the jury, witnesses who must have had more to say than was revealed by the police file, photographic evidence that was in conflict with the evidence given by the police at trial, timing evidence that was in conflict with the police evidence at trial, exhibits that were not examined and which may or may not still have been in existence, evidence as to motive or explanation that was improperly investigated and not presented at trial, and many other details which were simply in conflict with the conviction of David as it stood. In order to get to the truth of all these matters, we needed access to exhibits, previously undisclosed documents, the working notes of crime scene analysts and the pathologist, and so on.

But the cops wanted to dump these in the tip. They certainly weren't cooperating with us to put our concerns to rest.

So *David and Goliath* was a book of protest that exposed the Crown case for what it was — a series of inferences drawn from alleged facts that were not facts at all, and which simply did not stack up. The book was designed to put the case into the public arena, thereby forcing police accountability. Many people have said that the book did not convince them of David's innocence. It was not able to. Its purpose, which with hindsight one can say it ably achieved, was to expose the holes in the case against David, and demonstrate that unless those holes could be filled, his conviction was, at the very least, extremely unsafe.

When a jury considers its verdict, it needs to be convinced 'beyond reasonable doubt'. If, in any trial, the reasonable possibility exists that some other person was the perpetrator, even though that person may be unknown or not on trial, then clearly it is not possible to have 'no reasonable doubt'. If nothing else, *David and Goliath* raised the real possibility — on the basis of the evidence, not as heard by the court, but as known at the time of writing — that a murder/suicide scenario was more than a remote possibility.

As I have explained, the book came about as a result of Colin and I feeling helpless in the face of the lack of cooperation from anybody in authority — not just the police, but anyone within the justice or political systems. Now, though, the authorities could not ignore Withnall, Karam or the Bain case any longer.

David and Goliath was the fastest-selling book Reed had published in their 90-year history. The public and the media were in a frenzy over the Bain case. No doubt this was exactly the effect Colin Withnall had envisaged when he coyly said to me, 'Why don't you write a book about it?'

We had smoked the opposition out. It is a terrible indictment on the system that any element of it should be seen as the 'opposition' in a matter such as justice but, as I have learnt, that is the nature of the beast. The fact is that justice is a game, with winners and losers. You could say that a hung jury is a draw! The point is that as with all games, in order for a fair result all the participants have to play by the rules, and the rules themselves have to be fair. And therein lies the problem with our system.

So, yes, the police, in fact the state itself, was our opposition, our enemy. And while they were hiding behind the rules, saying that the game had been played, *David and Goliath* meant that there simply had to be a rematch.

The first tangible manifestation of this flushing out of the opposition was the announcement by Police Commissioner Peter Doone that the police would conduct an inquiry into what he called 'the *unfounded* [my italics] allegations in the book'. The purpose of this inquiry was obviously to clear the police of any impropriety! We, of course, were not interested in what the police thought of themselves. We were and are interested solely in getting justice for David Bain. In an ideal world, this is also what the police should have been interested in.

We had uncovered a considerable number of anomalies, contradictions and omissions in the evidence upon which David was convicted. These, we believed, were the result of a variety of deficiencies — an investigation that was bungled in the early stages; a premature arrest; faulty scientific analysis; and some deficiencies on the part of David's defence team.

We have never been interested in anything but the truth. What had amazed us was that every time we were able to peel back a layer from the superficial evidence, we began to see a clearer picture supporting David's claims of innocence.

But to get as close as we could to the real truth we needed access to source documents, key exhibits, and witness statements. Doone's announcement of an inquiry meant that some scrutiny would be possible, although we were sceptical, to say the least, that the inquiry would be transparent or far-reaching. We knew the police would only be interested in exonerating themselves, and shutting the door even tighter on David's incarceration.

Fortunately, Commissioner Doone was not allowed to get away with his masquerade. The PCA, at that time Sir John Jeffries, stepped in and insisted on the PCA's involvement in the inquiry. This was still less than we wanted, but at least we had a statutory body that was independent of the police involved.

The other benefit of the publicity the book generated was that key people began to come forward with information, or with offers of their experience or expertise. The irony of all this is that we would have preferred to have sorted out the problems with the case directly and discreetly with the police — hence my meeting with the Dunedin regional commander back in June 1996 and the commissioner himself in October. If that had happened there would have been no need for *David and Goliath*.

Chapter 4

Fighting on unexpected fronts

Mask of Sanity

Not long after *David and Goliath* was published another book on the case appeared — *Mask of Sanity*, by James McNeish. McNeish is an established author, who has written books on a variety of topics including McKenzie, of Mackenzie country fame, and Jack Lovelock.

Ours was not an emotional crusade based on nit-picking or technicalities. Our fundamental premise was that the jury did not hear the complete evidence, nor was the evidence presented in its proper perspective. James McNeish sat through the whole trial, and his book is largely based on what he saw and heard at the trial. To make my point I repeat a passage from *David and Goliath*:

> My sympathy goes out to the jurors who were asked to provide a verdict in one of the most serious criminal trials in New Zealand's history. They could reasonably have been expected in that natural Kiwi way to have been presented with the evidence in fair, reasonable and complete form, instead of the misleading and partial 'facts' that the prosecution presented.

Later in *David and Goliath* I list thirteen highly significant matters that we had discovered were not mentioned at all during the trial. That list has since grown to a massive size and is even more convincing — it is presented in detail in the 400-page submission we placed before the Governor-General in June 1998.

So in *Mask of Sanity* McNeish, for the most part, gives an account of the trial proceedings. Now I accept that a compelling case was made against David *at the trial*. McNeish bolstered up the case as presented at the trial with a considerable amount of mythical and psychological theory, and a few myths of his own.

His view, of course, provided great solace to the upholders of the establishment, and to the system itself. It also gave the media a different point of view to examine. But few, if any, saw past the superficialness.

McNeish's book was unfortunate because to some extent it impeded the progress towards David's eventual exoneration, by providing a platform for those who would like to see the system's foundations kept in place. The fact is, and I repeat it, that every plank of the Crown evidence heard at the trial has now been totally destroyed or shown in its proper perspective.

McNeish's great problem, as far as his work on this case is concerned, is that he does not exercise sufficient detailed analysis of the evidence itself. He accepts it at face value and then embellishes it with his own, in my view, extravagant theories.

Being an accomplished writer does not necessarily lead to intelligent analysis of minute detail. I would have regarded McNeish's book with respect had he confined it to the background information on the family that he gathered when visiting Papua New Guinea on the proceeds of a grant from the Arts Council, and an account of the trial as he saw it. Reading

McNeish's book again now, I quite enjoy his style and recognise the quality of the writing. Clearly, he and I are like chalk and cheese, both as people and in style. That should not prevent either of us from recognising the qualities of the other. So it is not on a personal level, nor on the basis of the quality of his writing, that I criticise his work.

At the time *Mask of Sanity* was published, I was of course asked by the media to comment on it, and also went 'head to head' with McNeish on many radio interviews and on *Holmes*. While the *Holmes* debate apparently pulled in a great audience, it was rather sad television I thought. At one stage I had to restrain myself from walking out. My main theme was twofold: first, that the facts McNeish was relaying were not correct; and second, that his psychological theory about David was totally unsupported and insupportable. For those reasons I referred to his book as a well-constructed myth.

At the end of the *Holmes* debate, as I was packing up my books and papers, McNeish leant towards me, with that rather unfortunate habit he has of getting right in your face, waved his finger at me, and said, 'You know, your trouble is that you let the facts get in the way of the truth.'

Such nonsense hardly demanded a response. Shaking my head in wonder that I had just wasted half an hour attempting to debate such a serious matter with him, I took my leave without speaking.

On another occasion McNeish made another telling statement, along the lines of, 'Mr Karam goes on and on about the police making blunders. Well, they may have made blunders, but it doesn't follow that they reached the wrong conclusion.'

Again, such a statement hardly deserves a response. But in the light of the blunders that we have now established beyond doubt were made, it is worth briefly exploring this point.

On the back of McNeish's book is a commendation by a Richard Mahoney, from the Faculty of Law, University of Otago, who is described as an 'observer at trial'. This commendation reads:

Mr McNeish speaks with the unique authority of someone who observed the whole of the Bain trial and conducted the extensive additional research detailed in this thoughtful and provocative book. It is reassuring that he reached the same conclusion as that of the twelve members of the jury.

On pages 52 and 53 of *Mask of Sanity*, McNeish refers to David's bloody fingerprints on the rifle, and comments:

What is not speculative, however, in the view of one who is attending the trial as an observer, Richard Mahoney, are the prints on the gun.

Richard Mahoney is a Canadian who lectures in the law of evidence at the University of Otago and as we walk out of the court heading for a coffee house in lower Stuart Street he says in his laconic way that New Zealand has gone to the dogs as far as crime is concerned.

'If David's prints are on the gun, that's it. He did it,' Mahoney says.

I'm unclear. A lot of confused elements are jangling in my brain, but I don't tell him this. I say, 'There's a lot of doubt out there.'

Mahoney: 'David says he doesn't remember. So what? He still did it.'

'You can't be sure. How can you be sure? A lot of people are in doubt!'

He laughs. 'I'm not.'

When paraphrasing the judge's summing up of the case (page 163) McNeish writes:

> He drew the jury's notice to the matter of the computer message; the accused's admission that he heard Laniet gurgling; and, *of particular significance*, the bloodied fingerprints on the rifle pointing to the accused — evidence from the Crown which 'ultimately you may conclude . . . has not been seriously challenged'.

The real facts about the fingerprints on the rifle are examined in chapter 7, and clearly demonstrate that this is one blunder by the police that not only caused them to mislead themselves, but certainly misled the judge, jury, McNeish and even, it seems, the erudite Mahoney. There are many more examples, but at this point suffice to say that all who attended the trial were bewildered by seemingly incontrovertible evidence which unfortunately was sadly flawed.

There are other minor matters in McNeish's work that have no relevance to the question of David's innocence or guilt, but are worthy of mention because they illustrate McNeish's thinking in bothering with such trivial matters.

On page 220 he comments on the other prison inmates' reaction to David. How he knows about this is not clear, but he states:

> The reaction of prison lags to newcomers can be revealing. At Paparua, David Bain met with savage humour after arriving from Dunedin. The inmates' response is best summed up by a conversation between the convicted child

abuser, Peter Ellis, and David Bain in a wing of the prison. At a chance meeting in the corridor, the following exchange reportedly occurred.

'Hullo, David.'

'Hullo, Peter.'

'David, I'll be your friend. But please don't treat me as one of the family.'

Peter Ellis was in Rolleston prison for his entire term. David Bain has never been to Rolleston prison. The two have never met!

The book is so full of inaccuracies and illogical theories that in the end it is undeserving of my respect. In an 'author's note' McNeish comments: 'Writers, like members of the jury, are enormously privileged — being granted the freedom and licence to interpret the evidence and the opinion of experts in their own and sometimes, in an original way.'

James McNeish certainly took great liberty with that licence. He asserts, for example, that David had a tattoo done on his left arm just days before the murders, and that the design of the tattoo had some deeply mystical and sinister connotations. In fact the tattoo was done over six months before the murders, and was simply selected from a variety of designs displayed in the tattoo shop. The design shown in the book is incorrect into the bargain.

McNeish asserts that David rather than Robin would have been likely to have used the computer because of the generation factor. 'Computers are a young man's tool.' In fact, there are numerous references on the police file attesting to the fact that Robin was a computer buff, and was passionately involved in setting up a computer network for small schools such as the one at which he worked. The jury never heard this evidence either.

McNeish also suggests that the only reference to Robin being interested in firearms came from David. In fact, once again there are many references in the police file to comments by Robin's friends, dating back to his single days, that he owned and used rifles for hunting.

In his psychological theories, McNeish ignores the testimony of the two psychiatrists who interviewed David thoroughly and attested to his having no personality disorders, and relies on two others who have never met David Bain! On that basis alone, it hardly seems worth commenting on. He seems unable to contemplate the fact that David's denial is not denial in the sense of refusing to admit something, but simply denial because he is telling the truth.

I shall quote one passage from McNeish's lengthy dissertation on his psychological theory — in which he draws on Greek mythology as well as all sorts of other unrelated and remote cases, including Adolf Eichmann, the Nazi responsible for the deaths of many thousands of Jews, and actually states on page 194 that 'my own diagnosis is guesswork'. The following passage is on pages 212 and 213, and includes a quotation from Dr Paul Mullen, an eminent forensic psychiatrist from Melbourne who thoroughly examined David Bain in November 1994 on instructions from Bain's defence counsel:

But here is a final puzzle. The murders occur not in 1993 when things are going badly for David but in 1994 when they are going well. 'He's succeeding in music and drama,' says Paul Mullen, 'he has for the first time a girlfriend. If he'd killed 18 months before it would have been easier to understand. Why now?'

The answer must be because the attempt to break from prison [the family home] simply reinforced the fact that he was still trapped. The attempt to escape merely highlights his dilemma — he cannot live with home and he cannot live without it . . . It is a form of transferred insanity and an illustration of the truth that a human being will go to ANY [McNeish's emphasis] length to obtain affirmation from another. And Margaret's needs — one bends over backwards to absolve her from blame — were strong and unmet.

The indications are that David, however, had he tried would never be able to break free.

At a gut level everything was still failing [the speaker is now the neuropsychologist, who has never met David and relies on McNeish for his assessment]. Poor kid — he never had a chance. What girl would marry him coming into that family. He's blocked. How could you bring a girl home to tea. He's in a war situation. In a war situation you're calculating to save your life. An analyst would go further and say that on a platonic level, the mother was having an incestuous relationship with David.

Her personality completely overwhelmed him. He's left with no sexuality. Castrated psychologically. He was actually doing something vaginally, in a symbolic way. And it was so complete he had nowhere to go.

I wonder if this guy really was a neuropsychologist, as his analogies seem to concentrate on lower parts of the anatomy.

The two psychiatrists who did interview David say exactly the opposite in their summation of him. Dr Phil Brinded, one of New Zealand's foremost forensic psychiatrists, who works extensively for Crown agencies, including the police, is a resident of Christchurch. He first met David just a few weeks after he was arrested, and as a result of David's imprisonment in Christchurch, has taken up the role of David's counsellor over the past five years. Dr Brinded has filed a report in support of David's pardon application in which, in layman's terms, he essentially says that he believes David was the finder of his family, not the killer. Furthermore, he has been unable to detect over this long period any symptoms of clinical psychological disorder. In this regard, Dr Mullen and Dr Brinded are in full agreement. Moreover, both have told me that they have never read such a load of hogwash as the McNeish psychological theory, which even he himself calls guesswork.

In fact David did bring girls home to tea. They even testified to that at the trial. Other friends visited him at home. He was not trapped. He participated widely in the community. He ran marathons, he successfully completed the Outward Bound course, belonged to the local sailing club, and also competed in orienteering events. He was studying three subjects at university and was voted leader of his tutorial class.

As time has gone by, *Mask of Sanity* has become inconsequential in our fight for justice for David.

The *Woman's Day* debacle

Another huge public debate arose on 13 May, less than a month after the publication of *David and Goliath*, when *Woman's Day* published a feature article entitled 'David Bain's Secret Life'. It was subtitled 'Convicted killer's kinky sex sessions', and promoted on the cover of the magazine with a photo of David and the caption 'David Bain's shocking private life'. The article, a four-page spread, was written by a freelance journalist, Chris Cooke.

This story is worth telling because it demonstrates not only the effect of the propaganda that develops around such 'cause célèbres', but also the number of fronts on which we had to fight to maintain our path to securing simple justice.

The basic thrust of this article was that David Bain regularly visited two prostitutes, who the article called 'Ruby' and 'Debbie', not their real names. They are quoted describing David's depraved sexual proclivities, and also as saying that David told them of reasons why he would kill his father, 'that his father had sexually molested him'.

On Monday 12 May, I was flying home from Dunedin. During a stopover at Christchurch I checked my cellphone, to find a message from David asking me to get in touch with him urgently. He sounded distraught.

I grabbed a taxi and went straight to Paparua prison. It transpired that Chris Cooke had somehow managed to get a meeting with David earlier in the day. He had slapped the *Woman's Day* down in front of David (it had gone on the shelves that afternoon) and asked him what he had to say about it. David, sensibly, refused to comment. Cooke then repeatedly asked him if he had killed his family. David again refused to reply.

David terminated the meeting, went to the prison authorities to find out how this guy had got access to him outside normal visiting hours (no mean feat, I can tell you, suggesting he was a highly inventive person), and called me on the phone.

David showed me the article when I arrived, and I read it in silence. I was stunned. I had just written a book and spent the last month proclaiming that David was a fine, innocent young man. Now this. Good God, I thought, no one would print this if it was not true. I vaguely recalled Michael Guest mentioning something about a similar story, and saying that when he checked it out it turned out to be a case of mistaken identity.

I looked at David. As always, he looked at me directly. He was upset, but level headed.

'David, is this true?'

'Absolutely not,' he said. 'I have never been in a brothel in my life and do not know any prostitutes.'

'David, please,' I said, 'recognise that this article is going to be very difficult to overcome. Fighting for your innocence requires not only a turning over of the evidence, but also a transformation of your perception in the public eye. I can only fight on the truth. All sorts of people go to brothels. There is not necessarily any crime in this; but I must know the truth!'

'I am telling the truth, Joe. I have never been in a brothel. I have no idea where this story has come from.'

We spent some time discussing the article from every point of view I could imagine. But he was adamant.

As I left to fly home to Auckland I was, for one of the few times in my then eighteen-month involvement with David, troubled with some doubt. Was he a pathological liar? If he could lie to me about one thing, he could lie about others. Are you being sucked in, Joe? That question began to nag at me during the flight home.

While I was driving home from the airport my cellphone went off, shattering my reverie. I knew I would be hounded by media from all over the country. I would have to comment. It seemed an extraordinarily difficult situation. If I said that David denied the entire story and I believed him, it would lend weight to the proposition that I would believe anything David told me and that I was no more than a misguided crusader, capitalising on his circumstances for personal motives. If I refused to comment, that would give tacit acknowledgement to the veracity of the story. If I made some oblique statement, that would more than likely just fuel the fire. What the hell was I to do?

The phone was still ringing. I picked it up. By now I was nearly home; it was about four o'clock in the afternoon.

'Hello, is that Mr Karam?' said a rather demure female voice.

'Yes, it is, who is this?'

'I am the person referred to as Debbie in the *Woman's Day* article, and I wanted to tell you how upset I am and sorry for David. It's not true, any of it. I told him that, but he wouldn't listen. I'm really upset,' she said, and I could hear the tears in her voice.

'Well, what is the story?' I asked.

'This guy kept hounding me with this story. I told him that it was a person who looked like David Bain. We now know that it wasn't David at all, and I told this guy that, but he wouldn't listen.'

I took her phone number, and told her to keep calm, talk to nobody, and that I would get back to her that evening.

What a twist, I thought. Is this a set-up, or what? But it did tally with my vague recollections of Michael Guest's mention of a similar story.

That evening my phone ran hot with media calls. I didn't answer it, letting them leave messages. Then, when I was checking the messages, the next bombshell hit.

'Mr Karam, this is the person called Ruby in the *Woman's Day*. I'm very upset. Please call me on . . .'

I called her, and she essentially told me the same story as Debbie. I could hardly believe it. What had seemed like an unmitigated disaster just a few hours earlier could now be dealt with quite conclusively.

I phoned Colin Withnall and explained the whole story to him. Colin is a man of action, and a man of integrity. He is also a very busy QC. Most of his work is highly intricate civil work, much of it relating to issues with government departments on behalf of large commercial interests. But he immediately saw the importance of dealing with this situation at once.

The following day, in the company of an independent lawyer, he took statements from both women which completely discredited Chris Cooke, and denied in total the contents of the article. One of the women lived nearly three hours from Dunedin. Colin drove all the way to see her and take her statement.

A press statement was prepared, and we agreed to go on the *Holmes* programme that night. *Woman's Day* were asked to participate, but refused.

The press statement read as follows:

On Tuesday, 13 May, Joe Karam was contacted by a person who stated she was the person named 'Debbie' in the article in the latest *Woman's Day* magazine which claims to have details of the so-called secret sex life of David Bain. 'Debbie' claimed that the contents of the article were untrue in many respects and that the author of the article had lied about his discussions with her.

As a result of this call, 'Debbie' was later interviewed at her home by C.S. Withnall QC in the presence of her partner and an independent solicitor who was present at Mr Withnall's request.

'Debbie' has stated that a few weeks ago she was telephoned by Chris Cooke, the author of the article in the *Woman's Day*, who told her he had been talking to 'Ruby'. 'Debbie' immediately identified 'Ruby' by her real name and Cooke acknowledged that she was correct. She said that 'Ruby' had been ringing her over the last three months stating that Cooke had been hounding her and she did not wish to say anything. Cooke then told her that 'Ruby' had claimed that David Bain had told her he had been molested by his father and that David had also told 'Debbie' that.

'Debbie' explained to Mr Withnall that 'Ruby' was a person who was well known to the people who worked in the sex industry in Dunedin as a person who told 'big yarns' for effect and to get attention, who convinced herself that her fantasies were real, was a 'non-credible witness' who even got confused between her clients. She went on to say that 'Ruby' had claimed some months ago to have had David Bain as a client, but 'Debbie' had told her that she was getting confused with another client of both 'Debbie' and 'Ruby' known as 'Stephen' who, in fact, required the kind of services described by 'Ruby' in the article, including being treated as a dog. 'Stephen', says 'Debbie', looks a bit like David Bain but is much shorter than David. 'Debbie' says that 'Ruby' had spoken to Michael Guest months ago confirming that she had confused David Bain with another person, but Cooke was now pressuring her with the story it was David Bain and she had been ringing 'Debbie' asking how she could get Cooke off her back.

A few days ago Cooke turned up at 'Debbie's home. Her partner was present and his truck was parked across the entrance to their property. After a discussion Cooke was told by 'Debbie's' partner that he could come in for a cup of coffee, but that anything said was to be completely off the record and that Cooke had no permission to repeat anything that was said. Furthermore, 'Debbie' would not sign anything. Cooke was accompanied by a young male who Cooke stated was a lawyer. This was reiterated a number of times throughout the discussion and accepted by Cooke. Cooke had already entered the property but the other male stayed out at the vehicle.

Cooke had with him two pieces of paper. One, an A4 sheet, was shown to 'Debbie' and her partner and was stated by Cooke to be the text of an article Cooke was proposing to publish. Cooke told them that he was writing the article to show David Bain in a compassionate light. The article, as shown to 'Debbie' and her partner, contained none of the allegations said to be made by 'Ruby' as to unusual sexual behaviour.

'Debbie's' partner directly challenged Cooke, saying that the article he was showing them was not the article he was proposing to publish and that Cooke's sole motive in publishing an article at all was to make money. Cooke did not deny either of these allegations.

The article shown to 'Debbie' did contain the allegation that David Bain had had sex with 'Debbie' at a Dunedin massage parlour. 'Debbie' says she immediately told Cooke that that was not true, and there were other 'pertinent points' that she noticed in a brief glance that were also not true. She says that Cooke told her that it was too late and that the article had already gone to print.

The other piece of paper was a short legal agreement which he was very insistent that she sign. She was told if she signed this Cooke and *Woman's Day* would protect her identity and pay her legal fees. If she didn't sign he implied that he would expose her identity and she would be in trouble with the police. He said on a number of occasions that the article was already in print and was going to be published anyway and that it was therefore better for her if she signed this agreement. She told him she was not signing anything.

'Debbie' further explained to Mr Withnall that she had once had a client who looked like David Bain who had a 'straight massage' (no sexual content) and that when she had seen David's photograph in the newspapers she had thought that it was David but was not sure. She had explained this to Cooke. She stated that if David Bain said that he had never been in a massage parlour in his life then she would accept that this client was not David.

She further stated that she had never told Cooke that the person she thought may have been David had told her he had been sexually abused by his father. She had made that assumption from something the person had said based on her own experience of sexual abuse as a child (but not by her father).

She did, however, state that she had known Laniet and that Laniet had told her of being abused by her father. She stated further that this was 'common knowledge' among the 'working girls' in Dunedin. She denied telling Cooke that Stephen had been abused, saying that she agreed with Cooke that if David and Laniet had been abused then it was likely that other family members had been also. She stated that Cooke had 'twisted' their discussions so as to show what was only speculation on her part as being statements by her made from her own knowledge. She said she had told Cooke that a lot of what she had heard had been through the 'rumour-mongers'.

She repeatedly told Mr Withnall that she actually knew very little, only what she had heard, but she had always believed that David Bain was innocent. She also repeated that she had thought the client she was referring to was David but could not be certain. She had told this to Cooke also, she said. His response was again to say that the article was already in print.

The meeting ended with Cooke being told to leave the property (in graphic terms) and that his story was 'bullshit and lies'.

Upon reaching the gate Cooke was heard to say to his male companion, who was still in the car, words to the effect that 'Debbie' had agreed that the story was correct, at which point she stated that there were a number of 'pertinent points' that were not true or words to a similar effect. Cooke told his companion that he would discuss those with him later.

'Debbie' and her partner both confirmed that the story in the *Woman's Day* was very different and very much longer than what Cooke had shown them, and that when they read it they were both extremely annoyed, so much so that 'Debbie' had telephoned Joe Karam to tell him what had really happened.

This statement has been submitted to 'Debbie' and her partner and has been approved by them. They will be taking independent legal advice.

Colin and I both appeared on *Holmes*, where we completely demolished the story and no doubt seriously damaged the image of *Woman's Day* in the process.

In addition, and without any prompting from us, the two women, independent of each other, phoned 4ZB in Dunedin and told them the truth, denying the story and discrediting Cooke and *Woman's Day*. As a result, Colin Withnall wrote to *Woman's*

Day demanding an immediate withdrawal and apology, at the same time reserving the right to discuss a damages settlement.

Woman's Day refused. They seemed to take the view that when a person had been convicted of murdering his family — despite his protestations of innocence and a well-publicised application for a pardon — it was open slather. How could you defame a person in that situation? seemed to be their logic.

For the time being, that was where the matter lay. We had dealt with the story conclusively. *Woman's Day* had come out of the matter in a poor light, while I imagine Chris Cooke would have had difficulty finding anybody else to buy his stories. At the same time, mud does stick, and ultimately, I told myself, the wrong would need to be righted.

In defamation proceedings a period of two years can lapse between the event and proceedings being issued. We decided the immediate priority was to concentrate on the job in hand, that of dealing with the police and the PCA so we could complete David's pardon application. This was duly achieved the following year.

In April 1999, just under two years after the publication of the article, Colin Withnall filed papers issuing defamation proceedings against *Woman's Day*. After a series of negotiations over a six-month period, the following retraction was printed by *Woman's Day* as part of an out-of-court settlement. This statement was also read out in court at the time of the discontinuance of the proceedings.

DAVID BAIN — RETRACTION AND APOLOGY

The 19 May 1997 issue of *Woman's Day* carried an article entitled 'David Bain's Secret Life'. That article was based on the statements of two prostitutes which claimed that David

Bain had been their customer.

In publishing the article *Woman's Day* carefully checked its sources and believed it could properly rely on them. However the prostitutes subsequently retracted their statements and announced they had been mistaken in their identification of David Bain. As a consequence *Woman's Day* accepts that the article had no basis in fact.

As a result *Woman's Day* wishes to apologise sincerely to David Bain for having published the article and for all the distress that it has caused him.

Woman's Day greatly regrets what has occurred.

No mention was made in the agreement between David Bain and the *Woman's Day* of any confidentiality regarding the out-of-court settlement. This meant that in addition to winning the battle, David was able to make it known publicly that he had won, and that in addition to the retraction and apology, *Woman's Day*'s owners, Australian Consolidated Press (ACP), had made a payment to him of $50,000. While in my opinion this let them off very lightly, it at least negated the costs and risks associated with litigation.

ACP were not happy when it became known that they had paid a convicted killer a handsome sum of money. Their senior management took the tone of a teenager who had been grounded, arguing: 'It makes it look as though David Bain has won.'

Well, you know what? He did win. And the reason was that ultimately truth prevailed.

Chapter 5

The Nicholas Greet saga

The saga relating to Nicholas Greet is relevant to the story of the Bain murders in a number of ways. It occupied a great deal of my time and money, and it remains a disturbing factor in the case. It once again demonstrates some sloppiness in the methods used in the original police inquiry, and it also shows the degree to which people, including the media, can get hooked into the maze of propaganda and innuendo that inevitably seems to surround any criminal 'cause célèbre'.

A month or two after David was arrested, Michael Guest received an anonymous letter in which serious allegations were made against a man called Nicholas Greet. The text of this letter is as follows:

Dear Michael,
I was a friend of several members of the Bain family, and I am also a friend of a person by the name of Nicholas Greet, of 56 Hunt Street, Dunedin.
    My reason for writing this letter is to express my concern at some comments that Nick has made over the past few months, and some that were made in confidence by members of the Bain family — namely Arawa, Laniet and Stephen.

<u>My concerns are</u>:

1. On Monday 29th June, Nick was able to tell me a lot of information regarding the killings before they appeared on the media. By 11 am he knew the name of the family and the street, the age of the family and that they had been shot. At 4 pm he knew that Stephen had died after a struggle and that Laniet was shot three times (this was specified).

2. When the ODT printed the picture of the position of the bodies, Nick was able to say that the position of the gun was incorrect.

3. I believe that Nick has made several visits to the house, and he removed a toy bear from the house in the week of June 27th.

4. Nick has mentioned to me that he has some sort of relationship with Stephen (sexual?). In fact I believe that he last talked to Stephen less than 24 hours before his death.

5. As I said earlier, I knew the Bain family, especially the children. The two daughters confided in me that at separate times over the past two years, they were having a relationship with Nick. I have talked to Nick about this since the shooting and he made reference to visiting Arawa on the night previous to the shooting (leaving around 10 pm).

Although I have no evidence that he was responsible for the deaths, I believe that Nick has a lot of information that could prove helpful in your enquiries.

Nick is in a delicate state at present, and writes a lot of his ideas and thoughts down in a read [sic] notebook. This includes all newspaper and magazine articles that have been published. This might just be part of his grieving, and would be normal if he was close to the family, but as he is telling people that he hardly knew the family, I believe something is wrong.

Nick has also made several comments about his belief that the phone is tapped and that his mail is being read by authorities.

I hope this information proves helpful, and if I can either think or find out more information, I will write to you.

I hope you do not mind my anonymity, but as I am friendly with Nick, and a lot was said in confidence, I believe that this would be safer.

Yours,

Helpful.

After receiving this letter Michael Guest interviewed Greet, but didn't make any progress. He then passed the letter on to the CIB. They called Greet in and interviewed him, taking a lengthy ten- or twelve-page statement. Although this included Greet's description of his whereabouts on the morning of the murders, the police did not check his alibi. Nor did they attempt to establish who may have written the letter.

By the time I became involved in the case Greet, along with his younger sister Rebecca, was a member of the committee formed by David's friends to fight for his innocence. Of course I read the letter on the file provided to me by Guest, and so was a little suspicious of him.

Greet's name also surfaced in an article in the *Listener* by Bruce Ansley, subsequent to David's conviction. Greet was reported to have told Ansley during the trial that Stephen Bain had told him just the week before the murders that David had come prowling into his room with the rifle during the night. But, according to Greet, Stephen couldn't recall whether this really had happened or whether it was a dream!

Throughout 1996 I spent a lot of time in Dunedin investigating various matters, and meeting with lawyers, witnesses and the police. I also spent a lot of time meeting with David's supporters. During this time Greet began to write me letters, which at times contrasted sharply with his statement to the police (which I had). He also called talkback radio and started a website on the Bain case.

One of the things Greet told me was that one day when he was visiting Stephen, at a time when David wasn't at home, the two of them had gone to David's room, got the rifle and the rifle key lock, returned to Stephen's room and fired the rifle out the window. The curious thing here is that at the time of the murders there were a number of spent cartridges in Stephen's room. Could this revelation of Greet's provide the answer? I wondered.

Although I treated Greet normally I was pretty wary of him, and only fed him information that was already publicly known, despite his attempts to get more 'inside' information. This annoyed him, and he became quite pushy when he realised that I wouldn't reveal my innermost thoughts, or open the books, so to speak.

So when I was writing *David and Goliath*, I surreptitiously laid a wee trap. I still didn't know, and nor did anyone else, who had written the Greet letter. Was it Greet himself, or was there someone else that he was opening up to? It seemed worth finding out.

In *David and Goliath* I mentioned the fact that Guest had received this anonymous letter, without letting on who the letter was referring to. I finished by saying:

I should dearly love the writer of that letter to make him- or herself known to myself, Colin Withnall or Stephen O'Driscoll. Absolute anonymity would be guaranteed. It is not that I place particular weight on the letter's contents, but it is another unsolved piece in the jigsaw.

Well, on 27 April, just eleven days after *David and Goliath* hit the bookshelves, one of the other Bain supporters received an email marked for the attention of Karam, Withnall or O'Driscoll. This person faxed it through to me early the following morning. When I saw it, I was dumbfounded. This is the text of the email:

Hi

According to Joe's book he wants me to get in contact with him. I am the person who wrote the letter to Michael Guest with regards to a conversation I had with a friend about the Bain case on 20th June 1994. I was hoping to hear something in the media that Michael wanted me to get in contact — but the first I have read is the page in the book.

I am unsure what information you want, but I (for personal reasons) feel that it is unsafe to give my name. If you want information I know that 'N' (don't know if you know the name or not) was going prior and after the 20th to David Best (Vicar, All Saints Anglican Parish) and Hugh McCafferty (Chaplain, Otago University) for counselling.

I will try to recap what I can remember. On Friday 17th I met 'N' in an agitated state coming out of the Aids clinic — for some reason he had test results which I don't know what they were. I remember him mentioning something about spending the night with Laniet (I think) and that 'she was

72

going to get it for what she had given him'. I have no idea what he meant. We talked for around $\frac{1}{2}$ an hour over a coffee and he left.

I next met him around 8.45 am on the 20th at Knox. For some reason he kept asking me if his hands were clean. I noticed that he had mud on his shoes and that there were wet patches on his clothes as if he had tried to wipe something off. I guess three or four in total. I remember that he was in pain and commented about some friends of his by the name 'Bain' had being [sic] killed. He mentioned something like 'Poor David'. I had heard nothing and didn't have a clue what he was talking about. It was only at around 10 am that I heard about the shootings, presumably a murder/suicide. I am working off notes that I have from 4 years ago so their [sic] will be gaps.

I met 'N' as he was leaving on the Monday and he was heading to David Best's — he had been previously on the phone to him. This struck me as unusual as Monday was David's day off.

I sent Michael some copies of Nick's diary entries dated from 16th June 1994 – 23rd June 1994. Nick left his bag in the common room and his journals were in them. As Michael could confirm the writings were of an extremely disturbing nature and I was surprised that it took so long before 'N' was interviewed.

I must say that I am rather surprised to see 'N' in the media all the time and so sure that David is innocent. One must wonder if he knows more than he has told the police — the journal entries pointed in this direction. After all, how else could he have drawn the place of the gun, and tell [told] me about the number of bullets etc prior to 12 noon

73

on the 20th June.

I will keep an eye open in the media if more info is required, but I feel unable to give my name at present.

This was staggering. Would Greet write this information about himself? If so, then surely it could only be the result of some kind of guilt complex. And there were some peculiar allusions, which really made me wonder whether he might be involved in some way that one could hardly imagine. On the other hand, if it was someone else, why wouldn't they come forward?

I faxed a copy of the email through to Colin Withnall, who agreed it was worth following up. So I packed my bags and was off to Dunedin again.

The first thing we needed to do was try and find out who had sent the email. Colin and I worked on this together for the next few days, with the help of local contacts in Dunedin, and eventually we struck gold. It was indeed Greet who had sent the email but, even more intriguing, he had gone to great lengths to disguise that fact. In fact, he had sent it from one of the computers at the university using a false identity, where he was a student of theology. Greet has been a student of something or another off and on for years.

At the same time, in what seemed a remarkable coincidence, I received a call from a young woman who had known the Bain family. She was frightened, she said, and desperately wanted to see me. I met her in the lobby of my hotel. Her story was basically that she had been befriended by Greet, but he was behaving very strangely. She was frightened of him, didn't ever want to see him again, but was too scared to tell him. While this added to the intrigue, she seemed so agitated and distressed that I felt I had no option but to take her down to the Dunedin police station for her own safety. I am sure they were extremely surprised to see me walk in! However, I explained the young woman's situation and left her in the hands of a female police officer who seemed as if she would treat her compassionately.

So now we knew who had sent the letters — the question was, what to do next?

We decided that passing the information on to the police would be a waste of time. And yet here we had a person who was virtually suggesting that he was the Bain killer.

For better or worse we decided to get him into Colin's office and see what he had to say for himself. As I write it seems like yesterday, when in fact it was nearly three years ago.

Colin began the interview gently, putting Greet at ease with a series of red herrings which made him feel important. Eventually we showed him the first letter.

'This is news to me!' he said. 'Never knew anything about this.'

He gave exactly the same response to the email message of just six days earlier. Total denial. He even tried to suggest that a colleague of his at the university may have sent it.

We explained gently that we needed to get to the bottom of this affair. Were we being mucked around by someone? Already this had occupied a week of our time, when we had other important things to do.

It was an extraordinary four hours. Greet steadfastly denied everything, even taking us down to the university with his Internet disk log, expecting to prove to us that he hadn't sent the email. He was on-line from just after 12 noon on April 27 until nearly 1 pm. The email was sent at 12.34. There was a gap from about 12.32 to 12.36.

Finally he admitted to sending the email.

'What about the other letter?' we asked.

'To the best of my knowledge, I did not send the letter. But for some reason which I can't explain, I might have,' he said.

When pressed for an explanation, all he could say was that he 'wasn't there on the 19th or 20th June of 1994'.

Now that in itself was interesting. Why would he mention the 19th?

In the end he clammed up, saying he wanted to see his own lawyer and get some advice. Of course we had no power to hold him, and so after four hours he left.

We were not much the wiser, except that we now knew the man was lying. But the question still remained — what was it all about? The lingering doubt that Greet knew a lot more than he was telling us remained, and in fact still remains.

During the interview we had offered Greet a drink of water, and so we had his fingerprints on the glass. We called the local CIB and gave the glass to them, for what it was worth, and we also called Police Commissioner Peter Doone and made him aware of the situation.

The police detailed a detective to investigate the affair, and we gave them the records of our interview with Greet. In the end they concluded that he was nothing but a harmless publicity seeker. What a very strange way to attract publicity!

Greet subsequently made a complaint to the privacy commissioner about the fact that we had videotaped the interview. This complaint was dismissed. He then made a public statement, saying that we had accused him of the murders. I must admit I was dumbfounded.

Greet himself, in correspondence with me, has confirmed that he keeps a diary on a regular basis. My understanding is that there are frequent references to the Bain tragedy which are quite alarming.

Whatever the real significance of Greet's actions, the fact remains that when he was first interviewed no effort was made to check his alibi, or to determine who had written the letter to Michael Guest.

Chapter 6

Cover-ups and cop-outs

Ladies of the night

As if I didn't have enough on my plate in the months following the publication of *David and Goliath* — what with the general media furore, the pending police/PCA review, giving speeches all over the country, trying to actually do the work of following up on leads and organising expert analysis, dealing with the *Woman's Day* story, Nicholas Greet, and trying to analyse and debate James McNeish's book — we were also inundated with calls from people who felt they had been unfairly treated by the police or the justice system. This included a number of Dunedin's ladies of the night.

There were two reasons for this. One was that Laniet Bain had been a prostitute for about eight months, so many of these women knew her and had information they wanted to pass on. But more often than not, the account I had given in *David and Goliath* of the police, and their actions with regard to Dean Cottle and other matters, had raised disturbing issues for these women with regard to their own situations.

Because it is not possible for me to identify anyone in these passages, and I have no absolute proof that what I have been told is true, I must preface this account with the caveat that I am simply relating what I have been told over and over again. To illustrate the type of story we were told, I will relate the account of one particular woman, who I shall refer to as Lady X.

This woman had been brought in to see Colin Withnall. She was disoriented and confused. She worked as a prostitute, and had done for a long time. At her first meeting with Colin, her information was so disjointed that it was not worth taking down. But in essence, what she seemed to be saying was that she was under the control of a member of the police. If she did not do what he wanted — which included being available for free sex with anybody he nominated — this man would bust her. He had various means of getting girls under his control, she said, including threats to run them out of town by refusing them permission to carry out their occupation, busting them on drug-related charges, and even threatening to harm or harass friends, family members and associates.

The final straw came, she said, when he wanted her to help 'get a judge'. With all the publicity going on, she wondered if Colin Withnall may have been the judge. Yes, she was certainly confused.

Anyway, my name came up during her meeting with Colin, and so a further meeting was set up. We went over all the same ground again, and then I talked to her for a while on my own. I asked her if she liked to read. She said she did, and that she'd heard lots about my book 'at work', but hadn't read it. She said she would like to read it, so I gave her a copy and she went home late in the afternoon. I told her where I was staying, the Southern Cross Hotel, and said if she wanted to talk any more, to get in touch.

My strategy was to gain her confidence. I have learnt that people like this become so disillusioned that they simply do not know how to trust anyone. That includes the police, their bosses, social welfare agencies, the courts, and so on. Often they don't even trust their own lawyers, if they have one, since usually there isn't much their lawyers can do for them, and they simply feel let down again.

Anyway, Lady X went off with my book, *David and Goliath*. About midnight that night she rang me. She was excited, but lucid. She said she had gone home, and had spent the evening reading the book, and was over halfway through it.

'So many things start to fall into place,' she said. 'I'm sure I can help you to put some pieces together. Can I please see you in the morning?'

She was much calmer and more clear than she had been that afternoon. She wanted to meet early, at 8.30 a.m. We arranged to meet at Colin's office. She would get a cab, she said.

Next morning I was there bright and early. By 8.45 she hadn't arrived. I rang her, and when she answered she sounded terrified.

'Why aren't you here?' I said. 'What's happened?'

'I can't come, I'm too frightened.'

'Who of?' I asked.

'I can't say, but you know. I know they are watching me, and I'm scared of what will happen if I come to see you.'

'Listen,' I said. 'If you come to Colin's office, nothing will happen to you. We'll look after you. They won't touch you if they know Mr Withnall is involved.'

'OK,' she said. 'I'll ring a cab and come straight away.'

Another half hour went by and she still hadn't arrived.

I phoned again. She answered but was now totally distraught and crying. 'They're here. I'm scared stiffed,' she whispered.

'Who's there?' I asked.

'They're here, the cops,' she said. 'They want to take me down to the CIB.'

'You just wait there and say nothing,' I said. 'We'll be there in a minute.'

We must have made quite a sight, a besuited, bespectacled QC and me running down the main street of Dunedin at 9.15 in the morning, then driving off in a great rush. We arrived in just a few minutes. I waited on the street, while Colin went straight in. Sure enough, there were two plainclothes detectives from the Dunedin CIB. Colin asked what they wanted of Lady X.

They said they just wanted to talk to her. They had been told to bring her in to the CIB.

'Is she under arrest for something?' Colin asked.

'No, she isn't.'

'Well in that case, please get out of her house,' Colin said, as he escorted them to the front door.

They got a second shock when they saw me at the door.

After they had left we made Lady X some coffee and tried to calm her down. She maintained that this was proof that either her phone or my phone at the hotel was tapped. They had heard her phone call to me the previous night, she reckoned, and they wanted to get to her before she got to me.

We then took an eight-page statement from her. Colin was going to Wellington in the next few days and made an appointment to meet Commissioner Doone. As a result a female detective from Wellington was sent down to investigate Lady X's allegations. Lady X, however, retracted a considerable amount of her story on the basis that she was confused and also said that the detective concerned had been 'role playing' and that she hadn't really meant it.

Of course not all the women who contacted us were in Lady X's predicament. Some had similar stories, while others were women who had finished with life on the game, and whose information formed part of our petition to the Governor-General for David's pardon.

Recently Tom Lewis, a former policeman, wrote an interesting book that is pertinent to the stories told by some of the women who approached us. During the mid-1980s, Tom Lewis was in charge of the serious crime squad in Dunedin. One of the chapters in his book *Coverups + Copouts* is titled 'Paedophiles, prostitutes, police and pay-offs'. It essentially relates the story of how his unit exposed and gathered the evidence to prosecute a sex ring involving underage women, police and prominent citizens. A commission of inquiry was called for, with over 5000 signatures being gathered in Dunedin, but this was squashed. Lewis says that he came into serious conflict with his superiors in Dunedin.

He eventually gave up the struggle and in 1987 resigned from the police and moved to Australia. He writes, 'I was still keen to carry on believing that one day the truth would out. Rather naively in retrospect.'

* * *

Other people who contacted us during this time included one of the men involved in the Wicked Willies nightclub case. The owner of the club had been charged with murder. I helped to sort out that case, and the charges were dropped (for more details of this case see Part II, chapter 11). The family of John Barlow, convicted of the double killing of Eugene and Gene Thomas in Wellington, got in touch with me. Barlow had three trials — the first two resulted in hung juries — and steadfastly maintains his innocence. During this time I was inundated with calls from people with stories of suffering at the hands of the New Zealand Police and the criminal justice system in general. Obviously I wasn't in a position to assist in most cases, but I usually lent a sympathetic ear and offered some words of advice when appropriate. On occasion people would send in copies of PCA reports and police files relating to their problem, which assisted me in building up my own understanding of the extent of the problem that exists.

There were other matters that ate up time and energy. My home in Ardmore, South Auckland, was on the market. TVNZ came to interview me about why I was selling, and turned the interview into a *One News* headline: 'Joe Karam says he's broke'. This falsehood caused my daughter, in particular, much distress. I instituted proceedings against TVNZ; after a series of negotiations they settled out-of-court.

In the midst of all of these events, though, I also made some other important contacts. One of these was Peter Cropp, a scientist from the ESR (Environmental Science and Research), which had carried out tests for the police, who was now working on his own account.

Another was a cousin of the Bain family who made contact with me, and had some very pertinent insights into the case. He had been in Dunedin at the time of the funerals, and said he now realised that there was a real chance that David had been rail-roaded by the police and some members of his extended family.

A Mr Sanderson, an opthalmologist who had given evidence at the trial, came to see Colin Withnall. He had some disturbing revelations and we took an affidavit from him.

I made contact with Dr Arie Geursen, the scientist responsible for overturning spurious DNA evidence which eventually resulted in the acquittal of David Dougherty on rape charges.

Finally, as things began to settle down, we were able to begin to concentrate on our primary objective. We gathered our papers and met at Colin's holiday home in Twizel during the first week of July 1997. During that week we compiled the first draft of David Bain's petition for a pardon. It would be nearly another year before it was submitted, due to the omissions and failures of the police/PCA inquiry into the 'allegations' in *David and Goliath*.

* * *

Among the many public addresses I made during the period after the publication of *David and Goliath*, to audiences that ranged from Lions clubs to ladies' dinner clubs to chambers of commerce, was an address to the Northern Club in Auckland on 9 June 1997. This turned out to be a significant occasion in the continuing drama that was my life at that time.

The man who thanked me and sat with me at the top table was Auckland barrister Robin Brown. For the most part my audience was made up of members of the legal fraternity, and in my speech I naturally talked of the Bain case and how it had gone wrong. I also touched on the David Dougherty case, of which I had some knowledge through my association with Dr Arie Geursen (for more details of this case, see Part II, chapter 14).

Just three months earlier, David Dougherty had been acquitted in a second trial, after spending three years in jail for the rape of an eleven-year-old girl. It was Arie Geursen who was largely responsible for providing the evidence that Dougherty was innocent.

In my speech I spoke of the need this exposed for criminal defence counsel to be far more vigilant than they generally were about the evidence presented by the Crown and the experts it called. In the Dougherty case, DNA tests done by the ESR for the Crown were incorrectly presented at his first trial and at his appeal. In essence, the defence had accepted at face value the integrity of the Crown's DNA evidence.

The Bain case, I said, had many similarities. That is, a lot of expert evidence was adduced at trial in a very misleading fashion. Defence lawyers, I said, needed to be vigilant in the extreme, obtain source documents rather than just deposition statements, and have them assessed by independent experts. In saying this, of course, I did not, and do not, excuse the Crown for effectively 'tailoring' the evidence presented to fit their case.

As I sat down after my speech, Robin Brown leant across the table and said, 'I was Dougherty's lawyer.' I was embarrassed and rather lost for words. Brown then added, 'But you were absolutely correct in what you said.'

Robin and I have remained on good terms ever since.

One of the other people in the audience that day was Tony Banbrook, a senior partner in one of Auckland's leading law firms. He had brought with him Allison Roe, the marathon runner; Banbrook was Allison's lawyer, and also a running mate.

Allison and I were to see a lot of each other as time went on, as she had recently separated from her husband. Naturally she became very familiar with my work on the Bain case, and she felt that I should be getting more assistance from the legal fraternity and the media over what she believed to be a miscarriage of justice. In January 1998, some six months after that breakfast meeting, Allison decided to do something about this. She sent a memo to Tony Banbrook, expressing her concerns, and inviting him to meet me. Banbrook was a senior member of the legal profession and had wide experience in criminal trials, from both defence and prosecution perspectives.

Allison arranged for the three of us to meet for lunch in late January 1998 to discuss the issue. Banbrook made no mention of the subject, pointedly sticking to trivial matters, so after some time Allison brought it up. Somewhat indifferently, and with a degree of what I would call disdain, Banbrook then asked me what it was all about, my belief in David's innocence, that is.

I told him that in the most simple terms, it could be put like this: 'The jury was misled on almost every point of significant evidence. They simply were not told the truth.' (At that stage, I still naively believed that was what justice was about!)

Banbrook's reply shocked me out of my innocence, and was probably the catalyst for this book, and my wider fight for justice in general. Smiling at me (an ignorant layperson), he replied: 'What's the truth got to do with it?'

Dumbstruck, I waited for him to elaborate. He continued, and although I cannot now recall his exact words, their essence was: 'Criminal trials are not about truth, old boy. That's not how the adversarial system works!'

I find it extremely difficult to dismiss such an abandonment of principle such as this. I have come to accept, however, that although not all lawyers are as jaundiced in their acceptance of the situation, most recognise that in our system truth and justice are not at all the same thing, and indeed are often diametrically opposed.

Chapter 7

The police/Police Complaints Authority review

As we have seen, soon after the publication of *David and Goliath* Police Commissioner Peter Doone announced that the police were to hold an internal inquiry into what he called the book's 'unfounded allegations' against the police. If he already knew they were unfounded, it is hard to see why he needed an inquiry!

When I was asked on TV3's national news for a response to Doone's announcement, I commented that it could be seen as both a good and a bad thing, in that an independent inquiry would be far preferable. Holding a police inquiry, I said, was 'a bit like having Richard Loe do an inquiry into foul play on the rugby field'.

What we had originally sought was a review which included a completely independent person, appointed perhaps by the Justice Minister, such as a distinguished former police officer, and/or an experienced trial barrister. In addition to examining police practices, it would consider the issue of David's innocence. This was not acceptable to the police! Hence, the writing and publication of *David and Goliath*.

The Police Complaints Authority (PCA), Sir John Jeffries, publicly voiced his disapproval of an internal police inquiry. Reading between the lines of the various press statements made at the time, it appeared that there must have been some terse discussions between the two parties, but the result was that the inquiry became a joint one by the police and the PCA.

Ostensibly, the PCA is an independent body which is completely separate from the police. It was set up by the government about ten years ago, for the purpose of responding to and investigating complaints by the public against the police. The Authority receives about 2500 complaints each year. It has the power to investigate complaints itself, oversee the investigation of complaints, and review complaints which are investigated by the police and sent to the authority.

All this sounds very reassuring, which it was no doubt intended to do by those responsible for its creation. In effect, though, what happens falls a long way short of what one might expect. The funding for the Authority is such that it has only one investigator! So what happens is that almost every complaint is referred back to the police station from where it originally emanated, for a delegated person from that station to investigate and report back to the Authority. The PCA seldom gets any closer to an investigation than reading that report. In high profile cases such as the Bain case, or Wicked Willies, for example, the police make a point of getting someone from another region to do the investigation for the Authority.

So even taking into account the best intentions of the individual who holds the office of PCA, in my opinion the PCA has simply become the police's single most effective public relations machine. It almost never finds any wrongdoing by the police, regardless of the circumstances. The police, for their part, can state proudly that an independent authority has found no evidence of misconduct or inappropriate action, when in fact the police have furnished all the material to the PCA.

For the Authority to properly carry out its statutory duty, it needs in the vicinity of thirty to forty investigators — but it gets funding from the government for one! This, of course, is ridiculous, even from an economic point of view. We continually hear that the police are short-staffed, yet at any one time a number of senior detectives are occupied conducting inquiries on behalf of the PCA. I do not know whether the police audit system provides a cost-analysis of this; however, with 2500 complaints per annum, it is certain that the cost is substantial. And then, of course, when they get serious cases, like those of David Bain or Wicked Willies, very senior people are tied up for a long period of time. If the cost to the police of investigating themselves was allocated to the PCA, then the Authority could function in a transparent and autonomous fashion, as it should, and the police could get on with what they are supposed to be doing, with a full complement of staff.

I suspect, though, for obvious reasons, that the police would fight tooth and nail to avoid this situation. In my opinion it is time for the commissioner of police and the Minister of Police to stand up and be counted. If we are to have a PCA at all, then let's have one that can perform the function it is intended for. Justice minister Phil Goff has recently announced a review of the PCA. It will be interesting to see how far-reaching it is and whether any substantial changes are recommended.

Since becoming involved in the Bain case, I have systematically and thoroughly examined the police files of some major criminal investigations. I have had extremely close dealings with Judge Neville Jaine, who took over from Sir John Jeffries as the PCA in 1997, over a long period of time. I have read many PCA reports on a wide variety of complaints. I have interviewed and met the complainants. My conclusions are simple — the PCA is prevented by lack of funding from being able to do the job it was set up to do. The police produce reports on themselves which the PCA can do little more than rubber stamp. Almost without exception, complainants are left feeling bewildered and angry, as the action which caused the complaint seems to virtually disappear altogether in the final report, due to a direct conflict between their recollection of events and those offered by the police.

In the Bain case, of course, the inquiry was not the result of a complaint. We did not make a complaint because we knew what the result would be. The police called for an internal inquiry for the sole purpose of refuting the allegations made in *David and Goliath*, the PCA insisted on getting involved, and it became a joint inquiry. Interesting corroboration of my view that, for the police, this inquiry was substantially concerned with publicly refuting the allegations in *David and Goliath* landed on my desk on the last day of the recent defamation trial. I received a copy of a letter on New Zealand Police letterhead from Ian Holyoake, assistant commissioner: crimes and operations at national head-quarters in Wellington, to the regional commander in Auckland. This letter was dated 22 April 1997, just six days after the book was published. The full text of this letter is as follows:

The Commissioner and some of his advisers have discussed today the question of quality control in major investi-gations. Police procedures have come into question in recent days by events surrounding the Bain and Dougherty cases.

The Commissioner will discuss the Bain case specifically with you on 23rd April, and I would like to make an assessment of the Dougherty case myself. To assist me to gain an appreciation of the Dougherty case could you provide me with a summary of the whole situation so that I can determine and advise the Commissioner on any action that may be necessary to preserve or restore our reputation.

I believe that the Auckland regional commander at this time was Brion Duncan. It was within days of the scheduled meeting referred to in this letter that Commissioner Peter Doone announced that Mr Duncan would conduct the internal police inquiry.

While I do not intend to cover the PCA report in detail, as that would require a whole book of its own, some comment is necessary to understand the saga of my involvement with the criminal justice system. The report of the inquiry was eventually released on 26 November 1997. It was entitled: *A joint review of the Police and the Police Complaints Authority of aspects of the Police investigation surrounding the arrest and prosecution of David Cullen Bain on five counts of murder.* Commissioner Doone was interviewed on national television and announced that it proved that the investigation carried out by the Dunedin CIB was indeed an exemplary one. The report, he told the public, was available from local police stations at a nominal price.

The report itself is 112 pages long, and it also carries an appendix by the Police Electronic Crime Laboratory of another eleven pages. We have since argued that major aspects of both reports are flawed. I found some of the report's findings so outrageous that I considered seeking a judicial review, but that course of action was abandoned due to the time and cost it would involve, and the fact that our primary concern was to lodge the petition with the Governor-General seeking a royal pardon for David. Nevertheless, between the report's release in

November 1997 and the lodging of the petition some seven months later, we forced the PCA and the police to reconsider some of the most serious issues.

David and Goliath was written with the dual purpose of provoking an inquiry into the circumstances surrounding the arrest and conviction of David Bain, and getting members of the public to come forward with information hitherto unknown. Now it may appear that the first objective was achieved with the police/PCA inquiry. However, this was not the case. In the introduction to the review it is stated:

> It is important we make clear that the focus of this inquiry has been on the conduct of the police in the investigation of these crimes and the subsequent presentation of evidence in court. It has to be understood that this inquiry and this report *do not purport to reach a conclusion on whether David Bain was correctly convicted of the murders* [my italics].

So it can be seen that this was not the inquiry we actually wanted. It did, however, achieve one of our goals, and that was to provide us with access to original exhibits, records and files hitherto denied us by the police.

The inquiry commenced on 12 May 1997. It was led by Assistant Commissioner Brion Duncan of Auckland, with Detective Chief Inspector Ted Lines of Wellington and Detective Senior Sergeant P.J. Mitford-Burgess of Auckland as his chief assistants. As we shall see, the police nearly got away with a complete whitewash, which the PCA would have been powerless to refute since it would have been relying solely on information provided to it by Duncan and his team.

Sir John Jeffries had written to the Bain defence team when the inquiry was set up, advising us that we would be contacted in the near future to discuss our concerns and advise us of procedures. Soon after that Sir John retired, and was replaced as the PCA by Judge Neville Jaine. By the end of June I had not been contacted at all by the inquiry team and Colin Withnall, David's counsel, had only had the briefest of informal meetings with Duncan in Dunedin.

I decided to contact the PCA to see where things were at. In response Judge Jaine informed me that the draft report had been completed! When I told him that I found this astonishing he asked me what I would like to do.

'It's not so much what I would like,' I replied. 'It seems to me that some very serious issues are at stake here, and it would be nothing less than a whitewash if the report were completed without any proper consultation with me. In fact,' I went on, 'because of the restraints in publishing a book, there are many other matters not in the book which I would like to canvass.' Judge Jaine then contacted Assistant Commissioner Duncan, who contacted me, and we arranged a meeting at the police headquarters in Auckland.

Police headquarters is on the fourth floor of a plushly appointed building, originally commissioned for the Auckland Regional Council and now known as the Vodafone Building. As I arrived for my meeting with Duncan I parked my car across the road and looked over at the big blue edifice. Here I was in my home town, I thought to myself, a good citizen with a reasonably high profile and a reputation that didn't have too many dents in it; a man who loved his country, was proud of its heritage and his contribution to it, and yet, in visiting the New Zealand Police, I felt as if I was walking into enemy territory.

I was early for my meeting. I composed myself and took a few deep breaths, waiting for the time to tick by. I don't want to be late, I thought, but not too early either. I smoothed down my suit, straightened my tie, took one last breath of fresh air, and in I went.

Up in the lift I went, to the fourth floor, where I made myself known to the receptionist. She replied formally: 'Yes, Mr Karam, Mr Duncan will be ready for you shortly. Please take a seat.'

And yes, shortly I was ushered into the war room. There was a huge wooden board table; walls set up with flow charts showing the procedure followed during the original police inquiry into the Bain family murders, David's paper run, and a number of evidential matters. About six people were at the table. Assistant Commissioner Brion Duncan introduced himself, then introduced me to his 'team': detectives Lines and Mitford-Burgess, his chief assistants, and others whose names I did not record, the computer programmers and analysts responsible for the raft of flow charts and other data on the walls.

There were no pleasantries. We sat down, Duncan at the top of the table and the others off to his left; me alone on the other side.

The meeting began with a discussion about David's bloody fingerprints found on the rifle. Mr Duncan said that blood from these prints was being tested by the ESR using DNA techniques to try to identify whose blood it was.

This surprised me as I had been under the impression that all of the material from these fingerprints had been used up in the initial tests done by the ESR at the time of the Bain enquiry.

The fingerprints referred to were highly significant, and had been cited by the police, both during the trial and since, as their most compelling evidence that David was the killer of his family.

The bloody fingerprints of David's left hand were located by the police on the forestock (barrel end) of the rifle and were what the police called 'positive fingerprints in blood'. That is, the blood had been imparted onto the rifle from David's fingers. Strangely, they were not in the position for holding and firing a rifle. Just the opposite, in fact: they were facing down from the top in a pick-up position.

It seemed to me that the police expected to confirm that these prints were in Stephen's blood, and that would confirm in turn that David had been involved in a bloody struggle with his younger brother and was therefore the killer. At the time of the trial it was not known whose blood had made these prints nor how old they were. I had made these points in *David and Goliath*. The prints had been identified as David's prior to his arrest just four days after the murders, but of course it was his rifle. You would expect his prints to be on it.

It soon became obvious during the course of my meeting with Duncan that I was wasting my time. Despite Duncan's civility, it seemed to me the team had taken a dismissive attitude, similar to that indicated by Doone's 'unfounded allegations' statement.

Immediately after this meeting I wrote to Judge Jaine, demanding a full and proper meeting with the inquiry team, in his presence. A meeting was then set down for the following Friday, 25 July, in Auckland. It was attended by Judge Jaine, and I also brought Colin Withnall up from Dunedin to attend with me. Remember that at this stage Duncan and his team had already furnished their draft report to the PCA.

In the interim I wrote a submission to Judge Jaine setting out an agenda of points that I wanted to cover. The meeting was a tense one, and it would be fair to say that Judge Jaine seemed to me to be mildly embarrassed by what had previously been submitted to him for signing off as the 'final draft report'. As a result of this meeting many aspects of the inquiry were revisited all over again.

By impressing on Judge Jaine the obvious fact that the police's draft report, far from being a genuine search for the truth, was no more than a 'destroy Karam's book' charade, we had forced the situation out into the open. At last we began to gain access to the many source documents that we had been denied for so long.

One thing that becomes apparent again and again throughout this saga is how often 'official' reports reveal only that side of the picture desirable to the agency in question. What is omitted is often far more salient than what is contained in a report. The only way of checking the true facts is to obtain access to source documents and material.

The first documents we had already obtained were the ESR documents from the original Bain inquiry, conducted at ESR Christchurch by Peter Hentschel and Peter Cropp. It was these that revealed the negative blood grouping results, and the highly questionable human serum results in regard to the bloody fingerprints. We were then advised that the police/PCA inquiry team had submitted many of the Bain exhibits to the ESR in Auckland, where DNA testing facilities were now available.

In addition the police, at our request, and I am certain under instructions from Judge Jaine, allowed us access to all these exhibits once they had finished with them. One of the strongest criticisms I had made in *David and Goliath* was that so much forensic testing that could have been done was either not done or improperly executed.

Amongst the numerous samples, documents and exhibits, we were provided with the murder weapon, David's rifle, which he, his father and his brother had used for rabbit and possum shooting. In anticipation of gaining access to this material, I had been to Melbourne to meet with staff of the Victorian Institute of Forensic Medicine and the Victorian Forensic Science Centre (VFSC). The purpose of this was to gain their assistance in having various samples, exhibits and Crown theories scientifically and independently examined. The VFSC is an Australian police agency, but at the same time it is a highly sophisticated unit employing scientists who are dedicated to the task of objective analysis.

Understandably, they showed some initial reluctance to become involved in a case which put them in opposition, if you like, with the New Zealand Police, and a highly contentious case into the bargain. However, I managed to convince them that there were real issues that did not seem to be properly explained by the Crown's theories, and they agreed to work for me. This was the only time, they told me, that either of these agencies had taken on a case that was not current, and in which they were not being instructed by an acting barrister.

And so, in due course, a large volume of samples and exhibits was despatched by the New Zealand Police, on my instructions, to Melbourne. Included among them was the murder weapon.

To recapitulate, the extraordinary chain of events in relation to the bloody fingerprints on the rifle leading up to this point went as follows:

20 June 1994: the rifle is secured as an exhibit on the day of the Bain family murders.
22 June 1994: fingerprint analysis of the rifle reveals four left-hand prints of David Bain on the forestock of the rifle in 'what appeared to be blood'.

24 June 1994: David is arrested and charged with the murders of his entire family.

August/September 1994: ESR scientist Peter Hentschel passes five
    samples of blood taken from the rifle to Peter Cropp, the ESR
    blood analyst. Cropp is able to get blood group results from
    four samples, the 'no result' test being on the sample labelled
    'Blood from fingerprints'. 'Ouchterlony' tests on this sample,
    to establish whether the material was of human origin, are at
    first marked inconclusive by Cropp, but then marked as
    positive by Hentschel.

May 1995: during the trial of David Bain the Crown, in a highly
    emotive manner, describes David's bloody fingerprints on the
    murder weapon as a supremely important piece of evidence,
    in both opening and closing addresses to the jury and also
    repeated by the judge in his summing up.

June 1995: David Bain is convicted on all five counts of murder.

July 1997: at my first meeting with him, Assistant Commissioner
    Duncan told me that there was some of this material left
    which was being DNA tested by the ESR.

August 1997: the rifle, after being subjected to DNA testing at
    ESR in Auckland, is sent at my request to the VFSC in
    Melbourne for testing and analysis.

* * *

So there I was in the Melbourne laboratory, all togged up in
white coat and protective gloves, with a group of scientists. Dr
Stephen Gutowski, an expert in blood and DNA analysis, was
responsible for logging in the exhibits and allotting each one a
reference number. Once all the items had been examined and
labelled we made a closer examination of exhibit 14, the murder

weapon. The ESR in Auckland had taken ten separate blood samples from this weapon. The first thing Dr Gutowski did was to examine the rifle with a special lamp that causes any blood to fluoresce, so as to ascertain where the blood was. To his astonishment he could not locate one speck of blood on the entire rifle!

This rifle was described initially as having been for the most part smeared with blood. When scientists remove blood for testing, they don't just wash it all off. They very carefully scrape just a small portion from a particular area and subject it to testing. We contacted the New Zealand Police, the PCA and the ESR in Auckland to try and find out how it was that the rifle had provided ten samples of blood just a few weeks earlier, and yet was now totally free of blood. I have still not received a satisfactory explanation from any of these agencies.

While in Melbourne I discussed with the scientists the various examinations that were to take place on the exhibits. These included bullet shells, bullet fragments, items of clothing, bedding, towels and the like. It felt like monumental progress to actually have access to this material, which had been brought about solely by the pressure placed on the New Zealand Police by the publication of *David and Goliath* some four months earlier.

Meanwhile, all I could do about the blood from the fingerprints was wait and see what the report of the police/PCA inquiry would say, because of course there was no blood remaining on the rifle for us to test. The report was finally published in a blaze of publicity on 27 November 1997, about seven months after the review was announced. It was a substantial document, comprising 112 pages, and yet not one mention was made of tests done on the fingerprint blood!

Once again the only way to find the answer was to go to the source documents. I wrote to Judge Jaine and got his agreement to obtain from the ESR in Auckland all the working papers in relation to the work they had executed on behalf of the police/PCA review team. This amounted to some hundreds of pages of file notes, along with photocopies of the test results. It took me about three weeks of solid work to digest and collate the information.

So, what did it reveal about the fingerprint blood?

When I received the ESR case notes it was revealed that in fact Hentschel had removed only two of the fingerprints, while the other two remained on the rifle. The ESR in Auckland took scrapings from these two and they formed what they called sample '3 + 4' from the rifle in 'fingerprints'. This material, along with the other eight samples of blood removed from the rifle, was subjected to DNA testing by the ESR on 7 August 1997 and again on 19 August.

During this procedure the DNA is first extracted from the sample material and quantified. This test is executed with what is called the Aces kit, supplied by Life Technologies, and is specifically designed to identify human DNA. A positive result means that the sample material is of human origin, and in addition provides the analyst with a measure of the quantity of DNA present.

On 7 August, all nine samples removed from the rifle were subjected to this test. The analyst recorded that six of the samples contained substantial recordings of human DNA, two samples contained a 'trace' of human DNA, and only the fingerprint sample '3 + 4' gave an entirely negative result.

For some reason the entire nine samples were subjected to the same test again on 19 August. I don't know why this was, although it is tempting to speculate. This test gave a similar result in broad terms, but could not be relied upon because the reagent blank, as it is called, which is the control sample, gave a positive result for human DNA when in fact, as the name suggests, it should have been clear of any DNA. Some form of contamination or other failure rendered the results of this second test useless.

Now, a 'no result' or 'negative' in the Aces test (as obtained in the first series of tests on 7 August) means that a number of possible conclusions can be drawn:

1. The test failed in relation to this sample only, but not in relation to the controls nor the other samples in the same blot or batch.
2. There is insufficient DNA present to give a result.
3. There is DNA present, but it is so degraded that it did not yield a result.
4. There is DNA present but it is not human.

Consider the following, as I did after I had studied these DNA results:

1. The fingerprints are in the reverse position from where they would normally be if the rifle was held in the firing position. They were more appropriate to a pick-up grip.
2. There was no mention in any police job sheet or forensic analysis that the bloody fingerprints appeared to be 'fresh' or recent.
3. All blood samples taken from the rifle for blood group tests at the time of the initial investigation specifically identified whose blood it was, except for the fingerprint sample.
4. DNA tests done by the ESR in Auckland identified human DNA in all blood samples from the rifle, except the fingerprint samples.

It now began to appear that in fact these fingerprints, described by the judge in his summing up at David Bain's trial as one of the most important pieces of evidence against David, *may in fact be totally unrelated to the murders*, on the basis of the 'no result' or 'negative' DNA analysis.

* * *

As I pondered these facts and tried to work out what all this could mean, once again my subconscious came to the rescue, as has often happened since I have become involved in this case. Early one morning in March 1998, at about 3 a.m. in fact, I woke with a start. I decided to go back to the beginning. What was the evidence put to the court during David's High Court trial in relation to the so-called 'bloody fingerprints'?

I got up and went to the stack of files. I found the chart of blood tests prepared for the trial, exhibit 614, and to my amazement discovered that the chart did not include those tests done on the fingerprint blood by Cropp and Hentschel. I then went to their case notes and made an analysis of every sample of blood removed and laboratory tested. The result — *the only sample taken and tested that was not included on chart exhibit 614 was the fingerprint blood!* The most important sample of all was not on the chart presented in evidence.

I noted that only *four* samples from the rifle are listed, when in fact five were taken, the fifth being 'blood from fingerprints'. My analysis that morning revealed the startling fact that the only sample tested by the ESR in Christchurch that was not in their official court exhibit was the fingerprint sample. This was astonishing. Could it be a coincidence? I asked myself. I rechecked my workings, and found that I was not mistaken.

At this time we were close to submitting the petition for David's pardon to the Governor-General. I decided there and then that if I could do one more thing before we submitted our petition, I would try to get to the bottom of this issue.

So I took my analysis, along with the DNA test documentation, to Arie Geursen, my DNA consultant, and arranged through the police and the PCA that he and I should visit ESR in Auckland to discuss the DNA tests they had done.

We discovered that a minute amount of the extract that they had tested with the Aces kit remained. It was so minute that it was debatable whether enough remained for any further tests. However, I obtained authority from the police and the PCA to have this remaining sample sent to Arie. He did not know whether any test existed which could advance the situation, but he consulted his colleagues, who in turn consulted a genetic laboratory in the US. It was decided that one test could be designed that may provide an answer.

Remember, the ESR DNA probe with the Aces kit gave a negative result. One of the possibilities of that result was that the sample may in fact contain DNA, but not human DNA; another was that DNA was present, but was too degraded to show up. A special test was designed with the assistance of the US laboratory which would cover a broad spectrum of mammalian DNA, including human, rabbit and possum DNA. The purpose of this test was to see whether any DNA existed in the minute remaining portion of the fingerprint sample which had given a negative result at the ESR when probed for the presence of human DNA.

By this time it was nearing the end of March 1998. The report of the police/PCA inquiry had been released in November 1997, and had completely supported the police handling of the original Bain inquiry. My most pressing concern was to finalise the submission we were preparing to put before the Governor-General, seeking a royal pardon for David Bain. The matter of the fingerprint blood and two other suspicious aspects of the police/PCA report were the final outstanding matters awaiting resolution before we could finalise our submission. I had been working full time for nearly two and a half years to get to the core of the many mysteries created by the various failures, ineptitudes and oversights of the initial murder inquiry and the police/PCA inquiry and report.

In the last week of May I went on holiday to New Caledonia with my then girlfriend. I needed the break and we had a lovely time. Needless to say I left my contact details with the DNA laboratory in case any news came through while we were away, and sure enough, one day a fax arrived from Arie Geursen. 'We've got a result, Joe; please give me a call,' it said.

Excitedly, though with some trepidation, I called Arie.

'We've got a terrific result,' he told me. 'There is a large amplifiable amount of DNA present in the sample . . . the fact that the ESR probed this sample for human DNA can only mean that the DNA we have discovered can only be some other mammalian species.'

I could hardly believe it. I told Allison, who responded, 'Joe, they'll just have to let him out now!'

After nearly a year of pressure and effort we had finally resolved yet another aspect of the case, and unravelled one more strand of the false fabric of guilt that had been woven around David.

We went down to the pool. We ordered a bottle of vintage champagne, and a large Churchill for me. There had been all too few occasions to celebrate in the last two and a half years. As I relaxed beside the pool in the warm tropical sunshine, sipping my champagne and enjoying the cigar, I reflected on the significance of the events leading to this moment.

I recalled how David had used this rifle for shooting rabbits and possums.

I recalled how damning these fingerprints had appeared to be to the jury who convicted David.

I recalled the chart of blood tests submitted to the jury, which included all the blood tests except those done on the blood from these fingerprints.

I recalled the police statements in response to *David and Goliath*, insisting that I had conducted a biased and superficial investigation into the case and that there was a mountain of evidence against David, his bloody fingerprints at the top of the list.

And I recalled my meeting with Assistant Commissioner Duncan of nearly a year earlier when he informed me of the ESR DNA tests.

And I thought of David, locked away for sixteen years for crimes he had never committed, as a result of totally flawed evidence such as these 'bloody fingerprints'.

Dr Arie Geursen completed a report on his work which is included in the petition for David's pardon, which was submitted to the Governor-General just a couple of weeks later, on 16 June 1998.

The whitewash

Earlier I commented that the police nearly got away with a complete whitewash. To demonstrate why I say this, I turn to the matter of the glasses lens, exhibit 172 at the trial, and photo number 62 in the book of photos presented at the trial. This piece of evidence was vital to the Crown case, as it was the sole physical link which they said placed David in the midst of one of the murders. The issue is the subject of an entire chapter in *David and Goliath*, called 'Needle in a haystack'. In a nutshell, Detective Sergeant Weir, who was officer in charge of the scene, gave evidence that he had discovered this lens in a particular spot in Stephen's bedroom on the night of the fourth day of the inquiry. Photo 62 was used by Weir to show the lens in the position in which he found it, according to his evidence at the trial.

In *David and Goliath* I alleged, with supporting data from the Auckland University Photographic Unit, that what Weir said was a lens in photo 62 was not a lens at all, but merely a reflection from a piece of plastic. 'No lens existed in the photo at all,' I said. Therefore, I contended, two conclusions could be drawn. Weir did not 'find the lens' where he said in evidence that he did, and a photo was produced which did not depict what it was said to, and which falsely supported his testimony as to where he said he found the lens.

The police have made great play of this issue, claiming that I have said the lens was 'planted' by Weir. I have never said that it was planted. I certainly do not say that in *David and Goliath*.

Anyway, we all get to the meeting on 25 July — the PCA, Judge Jaine; Duncan and his team; Colin Withnall and me. We begin with questions about the lens. Duncan proclaims with great gusto and confidence that we are wrong; Weir has been inter-viewed extremely thoroughly, he says, and is adamant that that is the lens, exactly where he found it. In addition, he announces triumphantly, the expert police photographer has conducted a thorough examination of our proposition, and disagrees with it entirely. Photo 62 is indeed authentic and what we claim, on the basis of analysis by the Auckland University Photographic

Department (one of the most modern and well-equipped in New Zealand), to be a reflection from a piece of plastic, is definitely the lens, Duncan says.

Judge Jaine is taking notes and observing hawkishly. Colin Withnall and I are astonished. Do the cops take us for a pair of total twits? By this time I have spent eighteen months and a small fortune analysing the evidence in this case, yet they seem to think we are a pair of nit-pickers trying to raise spurious doubts.

Well, we managed to convince Judge Jaine that at least he should get another opinion (and remember, the draft report already had Duncan's and Weir's version in it). We didn't make this up, we tell the judge. The Auckland University lab report is referred to in the book, and that is the expert opinion.

So Judge Jaine asked Duncan to get another opinion. Someone from police national headquarters referred them to a photo analysis specialist in Christchurch, Peter Durrant. Durrant had given evidence in over twenty cases for the Crown as an expert on photographic analysis, so Duncan sent Ted Lines and Peter Mitford-Burgess off to him with all the lens photos and evidence.

Durrant required a few days to complete his research. Of course, he had the benefit of the negatives as well, which we had not been allowed. When Lines and Mitford-Burgess returned for the verdict, they were dumbfounded to hear that there was in fact no lens in the photo!

What do we do now? Imagine the panic. Weir, who according to the commissioner had conducted a 'copybook' inquiry, had already given them a statement, which was already in the draft report to the PCA, verifying his original testimony!

Well, they decided they needed another opinion, so off they went to their old buddies, the ESR. Alas, even the ESR could not find a lens in the photo. So off they went to see Weir again, no doubt after a considerable amount of consternation and consultation. What he told them we do not know, because they will not reveal the contents of his statements or the answers he gave them. Apparently, he was interviewed three times.

Anyway, the final outcome is contained in clause 155 on page 63 of the police/PCA report. After a four-page preamble, in which a considerable detour is taken from the essential points, it concludes with this remarkable statement:

> We do not believe Detective Sergeant Weir knowingly gave false evidence or acted improperly in court. The outline in the photograph certainly looks like a lens *and we can accept that when the officer was sorting photographs for presentation at trial he convinced himself that here was the lens even though he had not actually seen it there at any stage* [my italics].

They then go on to offer what they call 'two possible explanations for the position of the lens', which I won't go into because the detail is excessively minute. Suffice to say that objective assessment of these 'possible explanations' by an independent expert employed by me renders them as ludicrous as the explanation for the evidence recorded above.

It is worth repeating, however, that had I not insisted on a meeting with the PCA the report would have concluded that photo 62 did contain a lens.

There is a final point that is worth making before we leave Weir, exhibit 172 and photo 62. The police were and remain paranoid about any accusation that evidence was planted. As I have already said, I did not state in *David and Goliath* that the lens was planted. I simply stated that it was not where Weir said it was, and that it is not in the photo that Weir himself produced to show it where he says it was. Despite all their efforts to refute it, even the police now accept that what I wrote in *David and Goliath* is correct. But interestingly, it is they who keep suggesting that I think the lens was planted. Even the report of the inquiry states that at the meeting on 25 July I was adamant it was planted.

Of course, as I have already said, all the police were concerned about was protecting their reputation; they were not at all concerned about the integrity of the case against David Bain. My concern is not whether the lens was planted or not. My concern is simply this: this lens was presented as very significant evidence against David; the integrity of that evidence has now been destroyed. My intention is not, and never has been, to make personal attacks on any person involved in the case. I have simply been concerned with examining the evidence. Unfortunately for the Crown, most of it does not stand up to scrutiny.

During an interview with Ian Fraser regarding the contents of *David and Goliath*, Dr Jim Sprott commented that eventually the Thomas retrial team overturned the whole seventeen points of evidence the Crown had put up against Thomas. He went on to say, 'It looks like Karam is going to do the same in the Bain case.' And so we have.

* * *

Another example of how deficient the review was also involves Peter Durrant, the photographic analyst from Christchurch. Remember that Durrant was recommended to the review team by police national headquarters. He was their expert, not ours. After he advised them on the lens, they got him to look at further matters. I believe that the vindication of our stance on the lens motivated Judge Jaine to look a bit deeper into our other concerns, the effect being that the draft report he had from Duncan was for the time being put aside.

At this point they took all the photos to Durrant and he compiled a very substantial report for them. He was commissioned by them remember, and had never met or had anything to do with us. He dispassionately and objectively examined a whole series of photos and video evidence, as it related to various issues either in my book or raised by Colin Withnall and I at the 25 July meeting. One of Durrant's particular areas of expertise is identifying shoe prints in carpet from photos. He has a highly developed computerised program that reduces a photo in specific ways to create the shadow left by a shoe in the carpet. The Crown had previously gained convictions based on his expert analysis and testimony. This particular science is known as 'equidensitometry'.

One of the issues the police instructed him in related to what the Crown at David's trial referred to as the incriminating luminol footprints that they said 'must have been David's'. In the course of that work Durrant made some interesting discoveries. He found impressions of the shoes *Robin* Bain was wearing that morning in and around the area where the gun and ammunition was kept, and also in the computer alcove room. He provided a booklet of various exposures to support his findings. Everything else he reported on was adverse to the police case against David.

The first time I heard of Peter Durrant was when I read the review report. On the very last page there are four paragraphs that make reference to his work, concluding with the statement: 'We are not persuaded by Mr Durrant's advice as it relates to shoe impressions.'

Durrant was extremely upset at this dismissive attitude to his

110

work, and in consequence made contact with me. He has since done a new report for us in support of David's pardon application.

Another demonstration of how the police deal with the truth relates to the meeting I had with Inspector Soper in Dunedin in June 1996 (my very first meeting with the police). Inspector Soper was the acting district commander at the time. We had a cordial meeting, in the course of which Soper commented that 'David's arrest had caused a considerable degree of polarisation within the ranks of Dunedin police at the time'. I repeated this remark in *David and Goliath*.

In the review report, clause 322, page 110, it is stated that Inspector Soper 'denies he made such a remark, and says there was positively no expression of disagreement among Dunedin police staff that David had been wrongly arrested and charged'.

The statement in the review report suggests that I am lying, that I made up the remark and attributed it to Soper. So let me put the record straight.

Prior to the publication of *David and Goliath*, I was interviewed on morning talkback radio in Dunedin. During that interview I made reference to Soper's remark. Clearly the police were listening to the interview, because within minutes a fax arrived which was read on air. The fax was from the Dunedin police public relations officer, and said in essence that although Mr Soper made the remark attributed to him by Mr Karam, the police wished to point out that once all staff had been informed of the reasons for David's arrest, there was no further dissension. I remember thinking at the time that Alec Soper had impressed me as a man, and I was pleased to see that he at least didn't deny that he had made the statement.

* * *

I could go through almost every one of the report's 332 clauses and make criticisms, but that would require a book in itself. However, I would like to make one final sally into the murky waters of this review. This relates to what is probably the most vital issue of all surrounding David's innocence.

There is a chapter in *David and Goliath* called 'The phantom murderer'. The basic theme of this chapter is that had it not been for the mistakes and sloppiness of the initial investigators, they would have known that David could not have been home at a crucial time, and therefore could not have been the perpetrator of this dreadful tragedy. I went on to say that those errors were compounded by the defence counsel during the trial, and a degree of non-disclosure and/or presentation of incorrect evidence by the Crown. Of course, all these allegations are found to be baseless in the police/PCA review.

The facts, in a nutshell, are these. In the Bain house, in an alcove adjacent to Robin's body, was a computer. There was a message on the computer which said: 'Sorry, you are the only one who deserved to stay.'

One of the few matters on which I am in agreement with the police is that clearly the murderer left this message on the screen. The police say David wrote it to represent a false suicide message from his father. I say it is the father's final message, his suicide note, in effect.

On the day after the murders the police called in a computer expert, Martin Cox, to establish the time this message was written. The message wasn't saved, so Cox could not check that time, but he was able to determine the time the computer had been turned on. He gave evidence at the trial that it was turned on at 6.44 a.m. on the morning of the murders. He was not cross-examined at all by Michael Guest.

Cox's conclusion from his examination of the computer relied on the taking of precise notes by Detective Anderson of the Dunedin CIB. Anderson made notes recording the times, according to his watch, at which Cox performed certain functions on the computer.

About 40 minutes after Cox completed his examination of the computer, he called the CIB and left instructions that Anderson's watch be checked for accuracy. This was 21 June 1994. On 24 June David was arrested. On 29 June Anderson's watch was finally checked, and found to be approximately two minutes fast.

This information was never passed on to Cox. Had it been, he would have amended his calculations and his evidence would have been that the computer was turned on at 6.42 a.m., not 6.44 a.m. In addition the Cox analysis did not account for seconds. Police advisors have since proven that a further 57 seconds needs to be deducted from the time, bringing it, in fact, back to 6.41 a.m. Cox was therefore briefed to give evidence which the police, somewhere in the chain of command, must have known was false.

At the same time there were two crucial witnesses who, believe it or not, were not called to give verbal evidence. Their evidence was read to the court. These two people, Tania Clark and Denise Laney, saw David in the process of completing his paper round. Clark said she saw David *walking* across Heath Street, some 300 metres from his home. Laney said she saw David about to go in his front gate. Laney is the critical witness.

Clark and Laney were interviewed during general enquiries conducted at the rest home next door to the Bain house, where they both worked. More detailed statements were taken from Clark over the next two days. Laney's statement was not taken until the following week, *after* David was arrested.

As you will see, two simple errors by the police on the first two days of the inquiry led to the entire process going off the track. It goes like this. In the process of interviewing staff at the rest home two other women, Tania Pratt and Linda Burck, were spoken to. Pratt said she came to work with Burck in Burck's *white* car, and that they travelled along Highcliff Road. Burck said she drove to work in a *red* car, and travelled up Every Street — that is, in the opposite direction! This peculiarity is not referred to at all in the police/PCA review report.

The original botch-up — that although Laney was seen on the first day, she was not interviewed until a week later — came about because in the course of transcribing the original job sheets from the handwritten notes to the data-processed files which are studied (or supposed to be studied) by the investigation team, the typist jumped from one name to another. Laney was missed out altogether, which led to the contradiction between Burck and Pratt's accounts of getting to work that fateful day.

Now I can understand a transcription error occurring. I cannot understand how the anomaly between the statements of Burck and Pratt was not noticed by the investigating detectives, which would have led them to refer back to the constable's original notes. This would have alerted them to the error, and to the witness Denise Laney! As it was, the only reason Laney came to light at all was that the following Monday (four days after David's arrest) the police conducted a road survey at 6.45 a.m. to talk to people using Every Street, and came across Laney on her way to work. It was then that Laney's statement was taken, in which she said she saw David arriving at his front gate at or just after 6.45 a.m. It should be noted that Laney was emphatic about this time, and her car clock was checked by the detective who took her statement.

Subsequent to the release of the report I managed to convince Judge Jaine that Denise Laney must have been seen during the week prior to David's arrest. It took five months of pressure before I finally received confirmation from the PCA, on 18 May 1998, of my belief that Laney must have been seen in that first week after the murders when they found the transcription error earlier referred to. I also insisted that she must have had a more detailed statement taken than the one on the police file. On Judge Jaine's instructions the police re-examined this proposition, after which they informed him again that I was wrong. Eventually Judge Jaine got Detective Lines to go to Dunedin to check whether there was any undisclosed material on the file.

Sure enough, a whole box of statements was found that had not been disclosed to the defence — among them, a statement taken from Denise Laney (the last person to see David before the discovery of the tragedy) just weeks before the trial!

So let's look at what would have taken place but for the transcription error, and the failure to check Anderson's watch (which should of course have been checked before he worked with Cox) until a week later.

On 20 June, the day of the murders, a detailed and substantial statement from Laney would have alerted the police to the fact that David did not get home until shortly after 6.45 a.m.

On 21 June, Cox would have told them that the computer was switched on at 6.42 a.m., some three to four minutes earlier.

Together these two pieces of information, which would have been known the very day after the tragedy, show that it was not possible for David to have written the message on the computer. He could not have been the murderer.

This series of disasters is compounded by another circumstance that may be more disturbing, depending on whose view is taken. It will be recalled that a box of undisclosed files containing a second statement from Laney was not found until May 1998. This second statement provided even more emphatic confirmation of why Laney was so certain it was 6.45 or later when she saw David.

Michael Guest, David's trial barrister, had permitted Laney's original statement to be entered into testimony without her giving verbal evidence, as he was afraid the Crown might have been able to get her to weaken on her stance on the time, possibly taking it back to before 6.44 am. (As we now know, this 'critical' time, when the computer was said to have been turned on, was incorrect.)

No doubt the Crown was aware of this weakness in its case, which is why it got Laney in just weeks before the trial, and took a second statement from her. Now nobody can say whether it was just an oversight that that statement was not provided to Guest, but it is certain that the fact that he did not know about it is extremely significant.

Had he known that there was no chance of Laney recanting on the time of 6.45 or later, he would have had no need to fear putting her on the stand. As it was, one of the three questions the jury came back with after five hours of deliberation was a request to hear Laney's statement again!

I reiterate, none of this information is in the police/PCA report, in which it is concluded that:

. . . the broad contention [Karam's] that the investigation was a bungled effort which led to a wrong conclusion being drawn and that officers then selected evidence to support that conclusion is rejected. We believe the original investigation was mounted and pursued with proper regard

116

to standards, policy and procedures and that those involved acquitted themselves with integrity.

All I can say is that in light of what is now known and what has been recounted in this book, all of which is confirmed in letters to me from the PCA, then I can not see how clearly this conclusion could have been drawn.

More importantly, the proposition that David was not home at the crucial time, which would have been known but for the bungling bobbies' botch-ups, is inarguable. There never would have been a controversy over the arrest, conviction and sentencing of David Cullen Bain, because he never would have been charged at all!

In relation to the trial itself, it is astonishing that Cox was not cross-examined at all. Michael Guest has conceded that his failure to notice the job sheet which recorded the fact that Anderson's watch was two minutes fast was a significant oversight, for two reasons. Firstly, had he put this fact to Cox, then Cox would have been bound to agree that the computer was actually turned on at 6.42, not 6.44. Secondly, as a matter of tactics Mr Guest could have set a trap for the police to demontrate that they had either deliberately, or negligently, omitted to factor in the difference in the timing. Mr Guest himself agrees that this point would have a significant effect on the jury, to David's advantage, severely damaging the credibility of the Crown case. As for Mrs Laney, the last person to see David before he reported the tragedy, her evidence was read to the court with Michael Guest's agreement. Remember, though, that in consenting to this arrangement he was not aware that Mrs Laney had given a more extensive statement to the police just weeks prior to the trial.

In effect, David Bain was deprived of the most compelling evidence supporting his claim of innocence, due to the negligence (deliberate or otherwise) of the police officers in charge of his case.

Chapter 8

The 'A to Z' of injustice

The petition to the Governor-General for a pardon for David Bain was finally lodged on 16 June 1998. It comprised some 400 pages, and the grounds on which it was based are as follows:

1. Incorrect and misleading evidence put to the jury.
2. Failure to disclose all relevant material to David's lawyer.
3. New evidence highly probative of David's innocence.
4. New evidence highly probative of David's father being responsible.
5. Incorrect and misleading arguments put to the jury, that is, inferences drawn from facts which were not facts at all.
6. Incompetent and negligent police investigation.
7. Errors by defence counsel resulting in an adequate defence.

We believed the petition demonstrated that the individual and cumulative effect of these factors led irrevocably to the conclusion that an innocent person had been convicted of the most horrific of crimes. We made the point that a retrial so long after the event, and in circumstances in which it would be virtually impossible to find an impartial jury, would be a waste of time and money. The only remedy was the granting of a free pardon to David Bain.

Some of the specific matters dealt with in the petition are outlined briefly below.

1. The Crown's presentation of a photograph in evidence which purported to depict an incriminating glasses lens in the position in which it was found by Detective Weir. There is no lens in the photograph. The photograph falsely represents the existence of this prime piece of evidence. This fact is now accepted by the Crown. In addition, the photo was added to the evidence only days before the trial and Detective Weir's evidence about the photo conflicted directly with his depositions statement.

2. A statement taken by the police just weeks before the trial, which confirmed David's alibi (that he was out on his paper run when the murders occurred), was not disclosed to David's defence; in fact, we did not obtain this statement until May 1998, and then only after considerable and lengthy insistence.

3. Two totally independent professional opinions (given by forensic pathologists) from Australia strenuously contest the Crown's evidence that Robin Bain did not kill himself.

4. Post-mortem notes made by the pathologist who gave evidence for the Crown at the trial which were not disclosed to the defence, and which were completely at odds with the evidence he gave; they also confirm the feasibility that Robin Bain could have killed himself.

5. Evidence from the Australian forensic scientists completely destroying the Crown's theory on the reconstruction of Laniet's killing. Laniet had three shots to the head. This was crucial, as it in turn destroyed the Crown's argument that if

David heard Laniet making gurgling noises, he must have been the killer.

6. DNA evidence that the bloody fingerprints found on the rifle — perhaps the 'clincher' in the Crown's case — were in fact made in animal blood, and were totally unrelated to the killings.

7. Evidence not called at the trial that David was not wearing any glasses in the days leading up to the killings (his own were broken and at the optometrists'). He would therefore hardly have needed to use his mother's old glasses to effect these killings in the dark.

8. I have obtained from the police photographs of the highly incriminating so-called 'luminol footprints', whose existence had been denied during testimony by the Crown. They reveal nothing even remotely resembling footprints. The defence says that it had been led to believe that these photographs were either over- or under-exposed. New evidence has been produced that even if the footprints existed, as testified by Weir and ESR scientist Peter Hentschel, they could not have been David's. They testified that they had measured the length of the luminol footprints, which they said were perfectly formed from the toe to the heel. Remarkably, they did not measure David's feet. They compared the length of the footprints to David's socks! These could not have been David's footprints, as when we measured David's feet they were found to be 300 cm long, more than 20 cm longer than these 'perfectly formed footprints'.

9. New scientific evidence from a forensic photographic scientist showing that shoe prints of the shoes Robin was wearing at the time of his death existed in the carpet in the area where the gun and ammunition were kept, and in the alcove where the computer with the suicide note was set up.

10. A number of statements confirming Robin Bain's highly distorted state of mind, and Dean Cottle's disallowed evidence that Robin Bain had been involved in an incestuous relationship with his daughter, along with several more statements confirming a belief that this incestuous relationship existed. This new evidence also corroborates Cottle's in that it confirms that Laniet went home that weekend with the intention of telling her mother 'everything'.

11. Evidence not presented at the trial that the detective who noted the times at which certain functions were performed on the computer, to determine the time at which it was turned on, used a watch which was subsequently found to be two minutes fast. This two minutes even more emphatically confirms David's alibi.

12. The discovery in early 1998 that the police had mistakenly transcribed a detective's notebook, and therefore failed at the time to take into account a very significant piece of evidence which also confirmed David's alibi.

13. A list of twelve instances where the defence failed to make points that were highly probative of David's innocence.

14. An affidavit from an expert Crown witness that he was instructed by the Crown to omit from his evidence a matter he thought was very significant. This matter, which related to the glasses lens, would have been very destructive to the Crown evidence if given.

In summary, these points demonstrate that during the trial the following occurred, all to David's disadvantage:

1. Evidence in support of David's alibi was withheld — either deliberately or accidentally.
2. Scientific evidence relating to the death of Laniet was wrong.
3. Evidence relating to David's bloody fingerprints was incomplete and wrong.
4. The lens evidence was false.
5. Luminol footprint evidence was false.
6. Computer evidence was false.
7. Evidence as to the likelihood of suicide by the father was incomplete and wrong.
8. New evidence was discovered by us which would have been discovered by the police had they not carried out a defective investigation.
9. Non-disclosure of photographs, statements and scientific working papers combined with other factors to create a false and misleading picture.

So there we have it, the stark reality of the false fabric of guilt woven around David Bain — a veritable 'A to Z' of injustice.

Part II

The criminal justice system

Chapter 9
What is justice?

The question 'What is justice?' is a familiar one. It echoes around the world in many forms — in parliamentary chambers everywhere, in the forums of the United Nations, even, in this electronic age, in living rooms across the globe as the latest sensational trial is reported from the US, Malaysia, or New Zealand. Sometimes it seems that justice has lost its meaning. Does it exist at all, or is it an outmoded concept to be debated only by philosophers?

In our society, we have traditionally placed great faith in our police and in our justice system. Despite cases like that of Arthur Allan Thomas, where it took nearly ten years for justice to take its course — ten years of struggle, lies, deceit, cover-ups, personal grief and sacrifice — we still cling to the belief that our country is one of the fairest in the world and our police among the least corrupt.

But is it justice when constitutional procedure prevails over truth?

Is it justice when the noble claim of 'innocent until proven guilty' is made laughable when an accused has been hung by the media before his or her trial has even begun?

Is it justice when a jury of twelve simple people are expected to divorce emotion from reason when deciding a verdict on the basis of 'beyond reasonable doubt' — a concept even the most learned judges cannot explain to them clearly — and when for the most part the closing summaries of both defence and prosecution are taken up more with emotional pleading than affirmation of fact?

Is it justice when the police are more concerned with protecting their own reputations than with ensuring that the innocent have not been proclaimed guilty?

The concept of justice has occupied the minds of great thinkers and philosophers throughout the course of history, and it is the principle of fairness and equality encapsulated in this concept upon which modern democracies rely. At the heart of this lies the question of law and order, or to put it another way, the individual's right to be treated fairly by fellow citizens and the state alike. The first and most famous philosopher to address the matter of justice lived some 2300 years ago in Athens. Justice to him was more than a concept. It was the precept on which decent human existence relied. Eventually he was put to death for his 'heresies', as they were then considered by the authorities. He was Socrates, perhaps still today the most celebrated philosopher of all time. Socrates' life was devoted to answering the question 'What is justice?' A quote attributed to him that holds special meaning for me is, 'If you will take my advice you will think little of Socrates and a great deal more of truth.'

Chapter 10

The 'Janine Law Syndrome'

Brian Kemp was born in East London in 1938. East London is not what could be called a fashionable locality, and Brian Kemp is not a fashion-conscious person. He is not the type to court popularity.

After leaving school Kemp joined the merchant navy. At the age of 22 he arrived in New Zealand, and after a short time he decided to join the New Zealand Police. His rise through the ranks of the police force was not a meteoric one, but after some ten years he became a member of the 'élite' group in the New Zealand Police, as a CIB plainclothes detective. Kemp rose to the rank of detective senior sergeant. He specialised in homicide inquiries, and for about ten years he conducted homicide scene investigation training schools at the police college in Wellington. He was directly involved in over fifty homicide inquiries, in many cases as leader of the team.

When Brian Kemp retired his police number was 380, which in broad terms places him in the top five percent of the hierarchy of the New Zealand Police. Unfortunately, despite his long and dedicated service to New Zealand policing, his involvement in a case which was not his own cast an indelible shadow over the last few years of his career.

On 26 April 1988, Janine Alison Law, an attractive and responsible young woman who lived in the Auckland suburb of Grey Lynn, failed to turn up for work. Her workmates were surprised at her unexplained absence, and rang the police. At 10.15 a.m., a constable went to her home and broke in to find her spread-eagled on her bed, dead.

An investigation team was set up under the control of Detective Inspector Plumer of the Auckland CIB. Plumer's team completed their work over the next few months, and concluded that Janine Law had died of an asthma attack. Inspector Plumer retired from the police the following year.

The coroner's inquest was held on 16 November 1988, some seven months after Janine's death. When giving evidence at the inquest, Plumer said: 'On a preliminary inspection of the scene and the body with other senior police officers, and from initial inquiries, it seemed likely that the deceased had died from an asthma attack.'

That view dominated the police inquiry throughout. DI Plumer's evidence concluded:

Although from a police perspective one must conclude that police inquiries have failed to fully establish the full circumstances surrounding the deceased's death, a stage has been reached that unless fresh information is received, further active police inquiries will not be continued.

After hearing all the evidence the coroner found: '. . . that the deceased died at her home on or about April 26th 1988, from a probable attack of acute bronchial asthma.'

The remarkable aspect of this case is that it demonstrates the propensity of the police to form a view and find it almost impossible to alter that view, and then, even more worrying perhaps, for this view to be supported by the police hierarchy even in the face of overwhelming evidence to the contrary.

Right from the outset, Janine Law's family, friends and lawyer contended that Janine had been raped and murdered. Their views (and, they therefore felt, they themselves) were treated with contempt by the police inquiry team.

So what was it that was found by the police on that first day?

Janine was found spread-eagled on her bed. The covers were lifted and her legs were spread wide apart. She was naked from the waist down. She was lying almost face down with both arms underneath her, and her pyjama top was tightly wrapped around her upper torso, seemingly restricting her arms. The pyjama top came to about the middle of her back, and below that she was naked. Seminal fluid was observed around the rectal/vaginal area. When the police lifted her head to get a better look at her face, it was noticed that she had blood issuing from one nostril, and her face was purple and blotchy as though she had been deprived of oxygenated blood. She also had a tea towel jammed down her throat. The police also noted there were some asthma inhalers in her bedroom. They failed to identify any point of forced entry into the house.

Within days, her family told the police that Janine was very unlikely to have been conducting casual sexual relationships. She was very prudent in her relations with men, and she did not have a current boyfriend.

They, and other friends, also told the police that although she had suffered asthma for most of her life, it was not and had never been of an acute nature.

The police, however, came to the conclusion that Janine had indulged in consensual sex some time in the previous 24 hours with a person unknown, and then in the process of suffering an acute asthma attack had, for reasons not supported by any medical opinion, jammed a tea towel down her throat.

131

The main point of this account is to demonstrate the unfathomable omissions associated with this inquiry, and the obstinacy with which the inquiry team stuck to their initial theory. This is a classic example of the way in which the premature forming of an opinion by any investigator can, and usually does, lead to a flawed conclusion. Brian Kemp calls the propensity of police investigators to do this the 'Janine Law Syndrome'.

Part two of the Janine Law affair began in January 1989, when Sandi Anderson, a lawyer representing the Law family, wrote to the police's regional commander in Auckland, Assistant Commissioner Brian Davies. Ms Anderson's letter strongly protested the coroner's findings. She also put forward a scenario that was, in fact, a remarkably prophetic description of what actually took place. Brian Davies replied, confirming and reinforcing the findings of both the police inquiry and the coroner.

However, as it transpired, a number of the junior officers involved in the initial inquiry were also far from satisfied with the result. One officer in particular, a Constable Dixon, was so incensed by what had taken place that he could not let the matter rest. Dixon had originally been the officer in charge of the body. Throughout 1989, Dixon suffered considerable personal anguish at what he was certain was a bungled and falsely concluded inquiry. He felt so strongly that he went to the lengths of preparing a case study on it, which he presented to a trainee detective course at the Police College in June 1990. Like Sandi Anderson's, Constable Dixon's analysis turned out to be remarkably accurate. It is significant that Dixon's analysis did not rely on any new evidence, simply the facts as known to the original inquiry team.

Five years later this whole fiasco became the subject of an inquiry by the Police Complaints Authority (PCA), at that time

Sir John Jeffries. In his report he wrote:

> If Constable Dixon can rightfully be given the credit for taking the first substantial step in the Police rethinking with his presentation at the Police College in 1990, then he also deserves credit for taking his doubts and uncertainties to the right man in the Auckland Police.

I wish I had known of the 'right man' in the police when I got involved in the Bain case!

The man Dixon went to was Brian Kemp. At this point Kemp's only involvement in the Law case was that he had been questioned, because he was known to be asthmatic, about the likelihood of Janine stuffing a tea towel down her throat during an asthma attack. He had said at the time that blocking one's breathing passage was the last thing a person would be likely to do in such circumstances! In effect, early on in the initial Plumer inquiry Kemp disagreed vehemently with the proposition that Janine's death was in any way related to an asthma attack. He provided a written report to that effect — that report disappeared from the file, and has never been seen again. Plumer denies it ever existed!

The PCA commented in its report that there was a conflict between the two which it could not resolve, and noted that some documents were missing from the files. It stated that while it had no evidence of any deliberate removal or destruction of material, it had never been offered a satisfactory explanation. The files all relate to matters that go against the findings of the Plumer inquiry.

In early 1991, nearly three years after the death of Janine Law, Constable Dixon took his report on the case to Brian Kemp. At this stage the coroner's finding of death by asthma attack was still standing, and had been supported by a subsequent inquiry by the Auckland regional commander, which confirmed the authenticity of the initial investigation's conclusions.

Brian Kemp read Dixon's report, and became convinced that the original investigation had been a botch-up, caused by conclusions being drawn prematurely and then clung to. He decided to do something about it.

Unofficially, but without going against procedural regulations, he obtained the Law file, which by then had been archived, and began his own inquiry. In its later report the PCA commented on Kemp's actions: 'There might have been elements of informality in his activities, but they were not improper.' Kemp compiled reports and notes of his findings and placed them on the Law file, now held in his office. Fortunately, he also kept copies of these findings at his home.

Not long after he began his 'unofficial' investigation, Kemp was issued with a directive to discontinue any involvement in the Janine Law case. At this time he happened to be going on leave, and when he returned the Janine Law file was no longer in his office. When he went to the computer to establish its status, he found that it had been 'B formed' — police lingo for 'lost'!

Kemp now began to find himself at serious loggerheads with his superiors. He maintains that there was a distinct feeling of hostility emanating from his peers and superiors — many of whom had been involved either in the initial inquiry or in the subsequent internal inquiry which endorsed its findings. While Kemp could not disobey a direct order, neither was he prepared to abandon the case. So, much to the chagrin of his peers, he doggedly pursued his inquiries in his own time and at his own expense.

Kemp completed a substantial report in August 1991, which subsequently has not been able to be located, and which his fellow officers deny existed. This report concluded in no uncertain terms that the initial inquiry was wrong. Undoubtedly, Kemp said, Janine Law had died as a result of being raped and murdered.

By this time Kemp was beginning to suffer personally as a result of the hostility to which he was subjected within his own office. He was excluded from meetings that he would normally be expected to attend. He was given the cold shoulder by people he had considered over many years to be his friends. He was made to feel like a pariah in the coffee lounge during lunch and tea breaks.

During this time Kemp lost nearly 25 kg in weight! He would arrive home in the evenings exhausted and distressed. But he would always comfort himself and his wife with the thought, 'I'm not the one doing anything wrong.' And so he persisted, in the belief that he was doing the right thing. It is what's known as integrity.

Eventually, when it became obvious that his personal efforts were going nowhere, he decided to voice his concerns to a colleague in whom he had faith at national headquarters in Wellington. He presented his report and convinced this officer that something was grossly amiss.

Finally, by 1993, some five years after Janine Law's death, Dixon and Kemp's conviction and persistence began to bear fruit. As a result of recommendations from national headquarters in Wellington, the Auckland regional commander, by this time Assistant Commissioner Brion Duncan, instigated a third review of the file.

On 22 September 1993, Duncan directed the Auckland city

district commander to order the review, which was carried out by an inspector from the Manukau district. At last, after five years, the file was out of the hands of the original investigators and the supporters of the bungled inquiry.

The review was to establish whether aspects of the initial inquiry had been improperly handled, to identify aspects that did not receive due attention, and how the police might recover the situation if fault were found.

This review came down firmly on the side of Kemp and Dixon. You could say, from simple observation of the facts, that it came down firmly on the side of common sense!

As a result, in June 1994 the case was reopened! Detective Inspector Rutherford was appointed to reinvestigate the death of Janine Law on the basis that it was a homicide. The result of this investigation was simple but spectacular.

Rutherford was instructed to reopen the inquiry on 2 June 1994. On 26 September, less than four months later, James Tamata was arrested and charged with Janine Law's murder.

DNA examination proved that the semen found on Janine's body was Tamata's. Tamata confessed and pleaded guilty to burglary, rape, sodomy and the killing of Janine Law!

The shortcomings of the initial inquiry were sensationally exposed. In addition to the bull-headed mindset of that inquiry, the issue of area enquiries and fingerprint work was raised. It will be recalled that the initial inquiry could find no evidence of unlawful entry. And yet, five years later, Rutherford's team established the point of entry (which Tamata confirmed in his confession) by observing a simple oversight on the part of the initial inquiry team.

The fingerprint expert had observed scuff marks and dirt from a shoe print on a downstairs window. The inquiry team had attributed these to the forced entry made by the first officer to arrive at the scene — but on the same files is a statement by this officer that he made no efforts to gain entry by any downstairs windows at all!

In its subsequent report the PCA commented:

If this approach [that here was the evidence of unlawful entry] had been adopted the point of entry would have probably been known right then and there, and possibly changed the course of the inquiry.

The early mindset of the police resulted in a lack of vigour in relation to other aspects of the inquiry. Area canvass enquiries were not extensively made, which resulted in a failure to establish that Tamata (whose record would have aroused suspicion) lived nearby. Five years later the Rutherford inquiry made more extensive enquiries which confirmed this fact.

It is my opinion, and the opinion expressed in subsequent reviews of the case, that both these oversights occurred as a result of the *mindset* of the inquiry team. They formed the almost immediate impression that Janine had died of an asthma attack, and closed their minds to obvious evidence to the contrary.

The PCA's report on the initial inquiry, and the subsequent police review, is scathing, while it praises the efforts of Constable Dixon and Brian Kemp. But by this time Kemp had had enough. He retired from the police in 1993, his long and distinguished career irreversibly tarnished by the events of the final three years of his service to the police.

At the time Tamata was charged he was in prison for the rape of another woman — this rape would clearly not have happened had he been apprehended for the murder of Janine Law.

No action was taken against any officer involved in this six-year saga. In fact, some of them still hold very senior positions in the force.

On 26 January 1996, Brian Kemp was awarded a commendation certificate by the New Zealand Police. Kemp says they saved the ultimate insult till the end. He maintains that he should have been referred to in this commendation as 'former Detective Senior Sergeant Brian Philip Kemp', rather than the civilian 'Mr' used instead. In police terms, he maintains, this says it all. For me, however, I see it very simply. There are too few Brian Kemps in this world.

* * *

The Janine Law case graphically demonstrates the problem relating to the pursuit of common justice in this country, when the opposition becomes the New Zealand Police. Inevitably, when a serious injustice takes place, the fundamental blame lies in the hands of the police. For it is the police who are charged with the gathering and presentation of evidence. If they get it wrong, then the entire process is likely to suffer, and they and they alone are in control of the evidence that is available to any court or jury.

In the Janine Law case there are two outstanding but unusual factors. The erroneous conclusions reached in the initial inquiry resulted not in the false presumption of guilt against a citizen, but the opposite — a guilty person remaining at liberty. This was not a case where the police could maintain the stance of 'noble corruption', whereby they at least gained the conviction of a criminal psychopath who deserved to be locked up anyway. The efforts of those who disagreed with the original verdict were aimed at catching a murderer, not setting one free.

But from the police point of view, that is not the issue. It seems that police culture is indelibly imprinted with the maxim, 'we are never wrong, and even if it looks as if we may be, we must fight to the death to avoid being exposed'.

The second unusual point about this case is that it was not a Jim Sprott, a Pat Booth or a Joe Karam who was seeking retrospective justice; it was a senior and highly distinguished member of the police fraternity! Significantly, their reaction to his efforts bears a remarkable similarity to the manner in which they have treated me! If you can't shoot the message, shoot the messenger. Get rid of incriminating file notes. Conduct internal reviews to bolster up the position. Conduct smear campaigns against what is perceived to be the enemy.

An interesting observation on what Brian Kemp refers to as the 'Janine Law Syndrome' is that the more we hear an officer in charge of an inquiry publicly state that he must keep an 'open mind', the more it seems to be demonstrated with hindsight that the mind is already made up!

The case of David Bain is a classic in this regard. On the first day of the inquiry the police referred entirely to the case as a murder/suicide (with David's father Robin the perpetrator). By the next day they were considering David Bain a suspect, and only two days later David was arrested and charged with the whole five murders. At this time David was strenuously protesting his innocence, Robin had not been eliminated as a suspect, no reconstructions had been conducted, no blood testing had been commenced, no motive or explanation had been ascertained (although a very serious one for Robin was on the table), and David's alibi had not been properly examined. Perhaps the most disturbing of these is that Robin Bain had not been eliminated as the perpetrator of a murder/suicide. It is axiomatic that, regardless of the instinctive qualities of a detective and his team, it should not be possible to precipitate an irreversible course of action before other possibilities have been ruled out.

The PCA report on the Janine Law case puts this concept most succinctly when it states:

> Furthermore it seems, although at this distance it cannot be proved with absolute certainty, an asthma related death was being seriously entertained on the first or second day of the inquiry. That perception did not fade in the face of further inquiries, *but grew against strong contrary evidence* [my italics].

It is remarkable how the mind of even the most experienced and intelligent investigator can convince itself of patently illogical conclusions when it is burdened with a prejudiced viewpoint from the outset. The whole point of being an investigator is to allow facts, and facts alone, to determine conclusions. Again I quote the PCA review of the Janine Law case in relation to the drawing of inferences: 'An inference is a deduction of fact that may logically and reasonably be drawn *from another fact or group of facts* [my italics].'

The Plumer inquiry concluded that Janine must have had consensual sexual contact with a person unknown, elsewhere than in or on her bed, and that she later suffered an asthma attack and died. The PCA report states:

> I must say that I have been unable to discover any evidence at all that would lend support to Plumer's conclusion . . . as

stated above. The objective evidence points to the *exact opposite* [my italics] of all those speculative propositions.

In the case of David Bain, at the heart of the so-called mountain of evidence against him were inferences drawn that either were not supported by available facts, or were the result of illogical rationale. The thinking process goes something like this:

We know that he's guilty (instinct). Therefore we can attribute other unexplained matters to him.

In order to support what he 'must' have done, it becomes necessary to overlook or discard evidence to the contrary.

In the Crown's summing up of the case against David, at a quick glance I can find fifteen statements alleging that something happened which are not supported by any facts.

The second disturbing feature that is demonstrated in the Janine Law and David Bain cases, and which is obvious to anyone who has been involved in or has followed cases involving police irregularities, is the manner in which the police as a body unite to protect even the most patently flawed position. I hardly need to repeat that it took ten years to overturn the Thomas convictions — two trials, three appeals, numerous police reviews, all of which found nothing amiss. Even when all the wrongdoings were finally exposed, there was no reopening of the inquiry, and no police personnel charged with the perjury and fabrication of evidence that they had been deemed to have committed.

The commissioner's attitude to my stance on the Bain case is a classic example of this. No attempt was made to examine the safety of David's conviction. The police have become preoccupied with protecting their reputation and hence trying to justify their mistakes or deficiencies. David's innocence or guilt has become secondary.

The case of David Dougherty is a further example of this. Dougherty was convicted of rape and imprisoned. He gained a retrial three years later, as a result of a petition to the Governor-General, on the grounds that the original DNA evidence was flawed. His was not the semen left at the crime scene, on the body and clothes of the victim.

Instead of putting up their hands, apologising and conceding the error, at the second trial the Crown contended that there must have been two rapists; only the second one left semen. This despite the fact that there was not one scrap of evidence — not one scrap — to suggest that two men were involved. Dougherty was acquitted. Only subsequently has a police review of the case concluded that he had no part to play in any rape.

So why this reluctance on the part of the police to accept and deal with mistakes in a fair and expeditious manner? They do get it wrong at times. When they do, it affects the lives of people in a way that unless you've been there, you'll never understand.

As a result of my involvement with the police over the last four years I have come up with two possible answers. I should make it clear that my assessments of these men are not as individuals. Brion Duncan seemed an eminently pleasant man, as did Ted Lines and Peter Mitford-Burgess, his assistants on the Bain review. In fact, as individuals, I do not know a policeman with whom I have a personal gripe. Which perhaps makes it even more incomprehensible that as a body they can be so obdurate when it becomes plain that they have got it wrong. This is even less understandable from a public perspective because policing, by its nature, does not represent to us a win/lose situation, but simply a need to 'do the job' in the best interests of society.

The first explanation relates to the nature of policing itself. By and large the police deal with the worst aspects of society:

domestic violence; crimes against defenceless women and children; carnage on the roads; alcohol- and drug-related activities. Basically they deal with evil; the evil of premeditated crime for gain, involving violence, drug abuse, booze, sex and general depravity. It is not hard to understand that this might create a siege mentality, an attitude of 'us against them'. This then leads on to the culture that has developed within the police.

Only a small proportion of the police make up the CIB, the crime detection branch of the New Zealand Police. These are the élite, the 'brains' of the force. Their mission is to solve crimes, and it becomes a matter of personal achievement to do so.

By nature these individuals are generally ambitious. Promotion depends on closure rates and closure times; that is, solving cases and solving them quickly. The more public the case, the more determined is the detective in charge to get an arrest and conviction, the more the police as a body feel they need to be seen to have won against the evil perpetrator of the crime.

In this situation it is easy to see how the ideals of justice in the purest sense of that word can become obscured, how once due process has been completed and the file closed, neither the inquiry team nor the police as a whole want their success revisited.

A second explanation can perhaps be found by taking an historical perspective. Until recently, the police have been their own watchdogs. Even now, with the Police Complaints Authority, by and large the police are only answerable to themselves. This perhaps leads to a subconscious feeling of invincibility. The internal nature of inquiries into police actions means that normal standards of public accountability are reduced to almost zero.

In the last few years, as a result of a less benign media, a more vigilant public, and a significant increase in violent crime, police results and methods have come under significantly greater scrutiny. Suddenly decades of self-judgement are being attacked from all fronts. The reaction, to stonewall and retaliate, is both unfortunate and predictable.

While an increasing number of citizens are sceptical, to say the least, with regard to the credibility of the police, it seems that those who could influence matters — politicians, the judiciary and influential business groups — are not. The police retain a feeling of invincibility, which is reinforced by the very people who should be their scrutineers. And so the culture becomes even more ingrained and self-perpetuating.

Chapter 11

The Wicked Willies case

Following the publication of *David and Goliath* I received numerous phone calls from people who felt they had not been fairly treated by the criminal justice system. It was beyond my power to do much about most of these, but there were two that I did become involved with, and which are worthy of attention. The first was the Wicked Willies case, which involved the death of Barry Coleman at the Wicked Willies nightclub in Christchurch on Christmas Eve, 1996.

The call I received came out of the blue on 24 May 1997. It was from a person who had been charged in relation to the incident, although he was not the person charged with the actual death. His name was Terry Brown.

The call went like this:

Joe, we desperately need help and don't know where to turn. Even our own lawyers don't really believe us. What happened was this. My mate Greg Mather owns a nightclub called Wicked Willies here in Christchurch. On last Christmas Eve, a party was going on at the club; everybody was drinking a fair bit and some sort of scuffle took place, a guy was knocked down the stairs and he died. Greg was charged with his murder, and we were both charged with attempting to pervert the course of justice. It's been through the depositions hearings and it's going to trial.

The point is, Greg Mather had nothing to do with it; he wasn't even in the room when it happened. We know who did it, but the cops are not interested. Greg and I are in an industry where the cops would love to get us, and I think they think this is their chance. We're going to go down in a big way for something we didn't do.

Naturally my first response was to ask what his lawyers were doing, and to ask for more detail about what actually happened. He said the police had a statement from the club's DJ, which was forced out of him, saying that Mather had done it. The police, and even their own advisors, believed that statement, he said.

I had a few phone conversations with Terry Brown and decided that he needed the help of a private investigator to gather evidence about what really did happen. I told him this could cost fifteen or twenty thousand dollars. I suggested that it might not be a good idea to use a Christchurch private investigator since he could well be a former member of the local police, and a mate of the detectives involved in the case. Brown agreed, and we decided that I should find someone. I contacted Bryan Rowe, an Auckland private investigator and retired superintendent of police. After talking to Brown he agreed to take the case, and went to Christchurch. After that my direct involvement was over, although both Terry Brown and Bryan Rowe kept me informed of developments.

So what actually happened in the case of the death of Barry Coleman at the Wicked Willies nightclub?

Around midnight on Christmas Eve 1996, after members of the public had been excluded from the club, a party took place for staff and a few friends. There were a couple of unsavoury incidents involving some off-duty doormen, and a couple of those on duty, in which Greg Mather, the owner/manager of the club, intervened. There seems to have been quite a degree of ill feeling about the place, in which excessive alcohol consumption no doubt played its part. Anyway, as a result of all this, Barry Coleman somehow got pushed, punched or otherwise man-handled, was propelled down the stairs, and suffered a broken neck. He died two days later, on 27 December.

Stephen Lane, the DJ, made a statement to the police at about 9.30 a.m. on that Christmas Day, and initially told the police that he did not know how Coleman had come to fall down the stairs. Lane then claims he was threatened by the police and had it suggested to him that Mather was responsible for Coleman's injuries. As a result, he made a written statement saying he had seen Mather push Coleman down the stairs. Later that day, at a social gathering, Lane told Mather and Brown what he had said in the written statement and why — namely, he had been threatened by the police. Mather said he had nothing to do with Coleman being pushed, and Mather and Brown told Lane to go back to the police and tell them the truth. For this piece of advice Mather and Brown were charged with attempting to pervert the course of justice because Lane went back to the police and told them that Mather and Brown had tried to get him to change his story.

After Coleman died, Mather was arrested and charged with his murder, and spent two weeks in custody. The police case was based on Lane's statement, even though it was in conflict with the versions of all the other people who were in the club at the relevant time.

Depositions, or pre-trial hearings, took place in March, in which a prima facie case was held to have been shown. The entire Crown case depended on the evidence of Stephen Lane, and without his evidence no charges would have been laid at all.

It was then that Bryan Rowe became involved. His investigations caused a total reassessment of the situation, and exposure of the true nature of affairs.

One of the doormen, who I'll call 'X', revealed to Rowe that he had been a close eyewitness to what had happened, that another person had struck Coleman a heavy blow to the head, which caused the fall down the stairs, and that Mather was not present at the time. Remarkably, X had gone with his solicitor to the police on 29 December and attempted to make a statement to this effect. The police chose not to believe him, interrupted his attempt to give a statement, and pressed ahead with the charges against Mather and Brown.

Rowe also, surreptitiously but legally, recorded conversations with the person whom X alleged had caused the death, in which the person admitted to having been the assailant. Rowe and the defence counsel for Mather and Brown presented this new evidence to the Crown prosecutor and the police, and so the police did what they should have done in the first place, which was to investigate the incident properly. In the process of this review, Lane recanted his statement that named Mather as causing Coleman's death.

The review revealed that the police had presented three quite different scenarios at the depositions hearing. Firstly, Lane said Coleman had rolled and tumbled down the stairs after being pushed by Mather. The detective in charge of the scene said Coleman was in a standing position when he banged his head against the wall at the bottom of the stairs and broke his neck. The pathologist said Coleman broke his neck as a result of a 'dive'-type fall down the stairs. Later the pathologist told Rowe that the versions of Lane and the detective could not possibly be correct. Obviously, if the police had properly interviewed the pathologist they would have realised that Lane was not telling the truth and therefore they had no case against Mather.

Two weeks to the day after the evidence gathered by Rowe was presented to the Crown prosecutor and the police, the Crown prosecutor invited Mather and Brown's lawyer to apply to the High Court for a discharge under section 347 of the Crimes Act on the basis that he would not oppose the applications. The applications were made and granted, which has the equivalent effect to an acquittal. Despite the evidence gathered by Rowe no other person has ever been charged. While the police were happy to lay extremely serious charges against Mather and Brown on the basis of the uncorroborated evidence of Lane, they will not lay charges (or have not at the time of writing in June 2000) against a person against whom they have the evidence of an eyewitness, and a confession.

Mather and Brown were convinced from the start that the police saw this as an opportunity to get them, and that they were determined to do so in face of any other evidence. While a PCA report into the case states that this claim could not be substantiated, one has to have a great deal of sympathy for it. There are a number of reasons for this, all of which the PCA report puts a benign interpretation on. Firstly, when the door-man, X, went to the police with his lawyer on 29 December to make his statement, the police did not want to have a bar of it.

It seems that a detective began to take down X's statement, but when it reached the point of naming a totally different person as being responsible for the death of Coleman, in the words of the PCA report, 'the taking of the statement came to an abrupt halt'.

The detective left the room and spoke to a sergeant. He then spoke to the officer in charge of the investigation, after which he advised X of the dangers of making a false statement. X then consulted his lawyer, and asked the detective about the process of joining the witness protection programme. He was told he would have to make his statement first. He then proceeded to make a statement, the contents of which were described by the police, the PCA and Bryan Rowe as nonsensical.

The aspect of this episode which rankles most with Brown, Mather and their counsel is that the original statement begun by X is believed to have been thrown out by the detective taking it, and the officer in charge of the investigation and the sergeant from whom he sought advice deny any knowledge of its existence. In addition, the detective who took it down did not record on his job sheet that he had done so.

The PCA report accepts that the two senior officers did know of the contents of the statement, and in effect explains the matter away by blaming its being discarded on the naivety of the detective who took it who, it says, made a serious error of judgement! The report goes on to say that the refusal to take the statement was inexcusable, and that had it been taken the investigation could well have mirrored that done some six months later by Bryan Rowe. It then states, and here, one might say, is the rub:

> For police to decline to take a statement naming a person allegedly responsible for a homicide when another person had been charged and was in custody merits censure. This is especially so when it was recognised at the time that there was no corroborating witness to support the allegation made by Mr Lane against Mr Mather.

Had it not been for the intervention of Bryan Rowe, it is likely that Mather would have gone down at least for the manslaughter of Coleman. Taking this proposition a step further, had it not been for Terry Brown deciding to call me and seek advice on what to do, and even more importantly, having the financial resources to employ Rowe, the charges would never have been dropped. Most people who find themselves in these circumstances do not have the cash to fight the police in the manner that Mather and Brown did. Their funds get burnt up on legal costs, and lawyers tend to fight charges on a negative basis rather than a positive one. In other words, their attitude is to try to undermine the police case at trial, by demonstrating that the charges have not been proved satisfactorily, rather than actually proving the innocence of their client.

This is understandable under the process by which justice is administered in this country. Lawyers are not meant to be, and do not see themselves as, investigators. They fight for their clients in the courtroom using legalese and negative tactics, and then rely on the whims of the jury system to bring down a verdict.

Imagine if David Bain had had the finances to have the facts surrounding the deaths of his family independently investigated. Instead of relying on an entirely negative defence, he would have been able to mount a defence that postulated the likelihood of a different scenario entirely. But our adversarial system does not work like that — when a person is wrongly accused, the system is hopelessly inadequate to deal with it.

The Wicked Willies case underscores the need for scrupulous investigatory work, particularly in the early stages of an investigation, because it is at that point that the foundation of the process is laid. The unhappy result of the Wicked Willies fiasco is that nobody has ever been charged with responsibility for the death of Barry Coleman. At the time of writing no inquest has been held into his death. The file remains officially open, and yet I suspect nothing is being done to resolve the case. Greg Mather has sued the police for wrongful arrest and recently reached an out-of-court settlement with them. This, of course, has a strict confidentiality clause attached to it, so we shall never know what he was paid, effectively to shut him up. It is reasonable to assume that he will have barely recovered his costs.

As for the police responsible for the fiasco, nothing has been done. They will either still be in their jobs, or have retired, or maybe even 'perfed'.

The PCA report is as contradictory as usual. On the one hand it strongly condemns the police, while on the other it finds no mal-intent or punishable behaviour. The ordinary person can only be left in wonderment.

The report quotes the questions put to the PCA by Mather's lawyer.

Why was 'X' leant upon to withdraw his voluntary statement of 29.12.96 implicating the new suspect?

Who ordered the destruction of that statement?

Why when 'X' made another statement that day which was patently untrue did police not say so?

Did 'X' or his counsel agree to or even know about the intention to destroy the statement?

Was it proper Police practice to destroy this statement?

On whose instruction was it that Mather's defence counsel was not told that the statement had been destroyed or otherwise misplaced?

Why was no job sheet made about the matter?

Why was the destroyed statement and its contents not discovered [made available to the defence] during the criminal discovery process?

In the very first paragraph of its report, the PCA contrives to deflect attention from the extremely serious implications of those questions with the following preamble:

> The repeated reference in the posed question to destroying a statement, in my view masks the real matter of concern which in plain terms is simply this. That when a person claiming to be a close eyewitness called with his barrister at the Police Station on December 29 1996 and there named a person other than Mather as being responsible for the death of Mr Coleman, why did the police choose to disregard this information?

The PCA has immediately deflected the thrust of its inquiry from one of possible mal-intent on the part of the police (non-disclosure of information highly probative of Mather's innocence) to one of explaining away the process by which it all happened. The point is that, regardless of the police view of the authenticity or otherwise of X's statement, it formed part of the information gathered in the process of their investigation, and should have formed part of the evidence disclosed to the defence.

Had it been disclosed, the defence may well have been able to have the charges against Mather dismissed at the depositions hearing. This attitude goes to the very heart of what is wrong with our criminal justice system.

The following excerpts from the PCA report are worthy of further discussion.

> Right from the outset I [the PCA] made it clear [to the policeman conducting the investigation on its behalf] that it seemed in this homicide investigation a potentially vital

eyewitness was apparently deflected from embodying his concerns in a written statement. I required a thorough investigation into this seemingly incredible situation.

To anyone with any knowledge of police practice, and who has an open mind, this situation is not 'incredible' at all! It is unfortunately not uncommon, and entirely credible.

The report goes on to provide some background to the situation with regard to X's attempt to make a statement. This information includes the fact that the detective taking the statement conferred with a sergeant and the officer in charge of the investigation before discarding the statement. The report states:

> The detective then said he discarded the one-page aborted statement in the rubbish tin. Counsel for Mr X does not agree with this. In any event the page was never seen again, nor was any job sheet ever completed recording its apparently brief existence.

It then goes on:

> Despite all the mitigating circumstances [for the police!] it is my view that it was a serious error of judgement not to take the statement proffered and follow it up with intensive investigation. It may have been a false statement. So what? I ask. In the circumstances of a homicide inquiry there could be no possible justification for simply ignoring it.
> . . . for the police to decline to take the offered statement was inexcusable.

As Bryan Rowe's enquiries revealed, this was not a false

statement. It is not incumbent on the police to decide what they want to hear and what they don't. But of course, we come back to my elemental point, which is that they already had a person in custody (Mather) and had already charged him with murder, *and they simply did not want to hear anything that contradicted that precipitate action.*

The report then says that declining to take the statement 'merits censure', and later, 'Ignoring X's statement may not in the circumstances amount to misconduct or neglect of duty, but it does amount to a serious error of judgement on the part of the investigatory team'. A little further on, it continues: 'it was clearly neglect of duty not to retain [the statement]'. And later:

> However, my exhaustive analysis supports the view [of the detective who carried out the inquiry for the PCA], namely that the disposal of the statement by the police happened because the detective who took it was acting in 'a naive and ill-considered way'.
>
> . . . Despite what happened then, I am not persuaded the evidence discloses an obsession [on the part of the police] to pursue Mr Mather and Mr Brown at all costs.

The PCA report highlights other deficiencies on the part of the police, including improper reconstructions, failure to acknowledge and accept the view of the pathologist, and failure to notice that the pathologist's view was at odds with the reconstruction of events proffered by the officer in charge of the scene. The report concludes: 'Having said this, I remain of the view that the failure had its genesis simply in a lack of professionalism.'

While it may be fair to accuse me of being more cynical of police conduct than the PCA, it seems to me obvious that had the police not acted precipitately in arresting and charging Mather, they would in fact have conducted the inquiry in a proper and thorough manner.

The fact is that no one, including X's counsel, Greg Mather and his counsel, Terry Brown and his counsel, and Bryan Rowe, *except the PCA*, seems to accept that the police actions in this case amount to anything less than a deliberate attempt to shore up the charges against Mather, which (however much the police may have believed in them) leads on to perverting the course of justice.

In my view, this report into what can only be described as a fiasco exemplifies my earlier point that the PCA stands as nothing more nor less than a false pillar of independence behind which the police disguise their unpalatable practices.

Chapter 12

'Wogs' —
fair game for bad cops

The case of John Joseph and Lindy Forbes came to my attention about the same time as the Wicked Willies case, in June 1997. Lindy Forbes was brought up in Christchurch, but like many New Zealanders she travelled overseas as a young adult. She met and married an Egyptian, and they returned to Christchurch to live in 1994. Her husband adopted an English name and in New Zealand was known as John Joseph. He is a devout Muslim, and Lindy has also converted to the Muslim religion since being with him. The couple brought one little daughter with them to New Zealand, and a second was born soon after they had settled here.

What John Joseph and Lindy Forbes had to say was quite remarkable, even to someone like me who had by then heard some pretty disturbing stories.

The Josephs arrived in New Zealand on 4 December 1994, and at first lived with Lindy's parents. Apparently they did not get on and, as a result, the couple moved out three months later.

Now John Joseph is a very well educated and intelligent man. He had obtained four degrees in Egypt, including an LLB (bachelor of law) and a bachelor of commerce and marketing. His law degree did not qualify him to practise law in New Zealand, but his commerce degree was recognised by the New Zealand Qualifications Authority. He had set up a consulting business which he ran from home, advising immigrants on getting businesses started in New Zealand. He was also an accomplished linguist, fluent in Arabic, French, Spanish and English. He did some work as an interpreter, on occasion for the New Zealand Police.

John Joseph's real troubles in New Zealand began during the early hours of 14 June 1996. As he was driving home at about midnight a police car, its lights flashing, ordered him to pull over. As he did so, the traffic lights in front of him turned orange or red, depending on whose version you believe, his or the police. He stopped immediately after going through the lights, got out of the car, and showed the police his licence. They asked him to blow in the bag, which he readily agreed to, saying, 'That will be no problem as I am a Muslim, and never drink alcohol.' Sure enough, the crystals did not change colour. The police, however, were apparently not satisfied, and asked him to accompany them to the police station. Joseph locked his car, and peacefully went with them.

It is at this point that the account starts to become rather murky, because John Joseph's version of events contrasts sharply with that of the police who were present, and in addition, the police themselves have presented several wildly conflicting statements.

However, there are some things which are simply a matter of fact. At about 1.30 a.m. they arrived at Christchurch Central Police Station. There were four police officers in attendance when Joseph was taken into the police station, two from the car that had apprehended him, and two behind the desk. He was not charged with anything, nor was he under arrest, but on arrival he was requested to empty his pockets and take off his belt. At this point he objected and became verbally aggressive. According to him, that was when the fun started.

Joseph denies laying a hand on any policeman at any stage. In fact Joseph is a little chap, standing about 1.6 metres tall and weighing about 55 kg. With four cops present, it is difficult to imagine how he could have done much damage even if he had tried.

According to Joseph's statement, when he refused to take off his belt, or at least demanded to know why he should, one of the police replied along the lines of: 'You little bastard, just do what you're told, you fucking wog.' At this point Joseph lost his cool and replied, 'If you think I'm a fucking wog, then you are a white pig.'

Joseph was then forced to the ground and handcuffed.

It is almost impossible to determine what actually took place over the next two hours. Joseph was apparently locked up in a cell, taken out of the cell, asked to give a blood sample, and refused. At about 3.00 a.m., Lindy received a phone call from the police to say that they were holding her husband, who was drunk and disorderly, and could she come down to the station. Somewhat mystified, since she knew her husband did not drink, she gathered up her two young children and took a taxi to the police station. What she found when she arrived completely shocked her — a bloody, battered mess, who had difficulty breathing, had stitches on his face, and could not walk!

John Joseph spent eight hours in hospital the following day — his medical records show that he was suffering from a broken ankle, which required a cast, two fractured ribs, a fractured right eye socket, a chipped tooth, internal bleeding in his left eye, a laceration under his chin, severe bruising to his throat and neck, and general bruising over the rest of his body.

Joseph alleges that not only was he punched and belted by

two police officers, but that they also repeatedly kicked him while he was handcuffed and lying on the ground. His injuries tend to support his allegations. At the subsequent trial, the police produced no medical evidence of any injuries they had suffered, but claimed that one of the police officers had suffered bruising to his face.

The day after these events took place Joseph made a complaint to the PCA. The familiar scenario unfolded, whereby a senior sergeant from the Christchurch police attended and took an eleven-page statement from him.

Joseph was subsequently charged by the police with refusing to give a blood specimen, assaulting two police officers, and driving through a red light. His trial took place in the Christchurch District Court on 29 and 30 October 1996, just three and a half months later. Without going into details of the evidence given at the trial, suffice to say that the court was presented with two totally conflicting accounts of what took place in the early hours of 14 June.

Joseph was convicted on all charges. For refusing to give a blood sample he was fined $900 and disqualified from driving for twelve months. He was fined $400 for assaulting one police officer and $300 for assaulting the other. For driving through a red light he was fined $75.

John Joseph was not a man to lie down in the face of what he considered to be a severe miscarriage of justice. He believed that he had been beaten up unnecessarily and then, to add insult to injury, convicted of beating up those who had injured him. He began a deluge of letters of complaint to every imaginable person — the PCA, the Crown Law Office, MPs, the police themselves. His letters and their replies fill volumes of Eastlight ringbinders. He also lodged an appeal against his convictions, which was heard in the Christchurch High Court before Justice Hansen on 26 February 1997.

In his time in New Zealand Joseph had built up quite a network of friends and associates, who now formed a support group for him and his family. One of the reasons these people were so convinced of his innocence was that they all knew he never drank alcohol because of his religion. Yet all the police at his trial maintained that he smelt of alcohol, and they even alleged that he told them he had that evening drunk a whole cask of wine! This despite evidence called in his defence from the people he had been visiting, who testified that he had not drunk any alcohol that night.

His support group included some quite prominent people, including a local MP; Dr Ron Macintyre QSM, of Canterbury University's Political Science Unit; Richard Thomson, a retired university lecturer in psychology and sociology; Dr Bruce Harding, an educator at Christchurch Boys High School and the curator of Ngaio Marsh House; and even a former police officer, Ron Moncur, who had had dealings with Joseph in Egypt when there on a business trip. Many of these people provided testimonials attesting to his good character. It must have become clear to the police that Joseph was not going to give up, and that he had a considerable amount of articulate, intelligent and persuasive support.

On 21 November 1996, three weeks after his trial, seven police turned up out of the blue at his house with a search warrant. He was charged with sexual offences against one of his neighbours, offences which had allegedly taken place in July. Six days later, on 27 November, four police officers turned up at the Josephs' house, served a trespass notice on Lindy, and took Joseph in to the police station to answer charges of sexual offences laid by another woman, and alleged to have taken place the previous March.

On 22 January 1997 Lindy was arrested and held for three hours in a cell, and charged with perverting the course of justice. She had spoken with one of the women involved in the rape charges against her husband, pleading with her that her husband John Joseph was innocent.

Throughout this time a number of other bizarre events are alleged to have taken place. While these are somewhat peripheral to the charges that were laid, they nevertheless indicate the degree of distress being suffered by the Josephs at this time.

John Joseph had been beaten up in Christchurch by two men he had never seen before. The police filed charges very reluctantly it seems, and when the prosecution eventually took place it failed.

On 4 December, Joseph was listening to the radio while his wife was on the phone. Suddenly Lindy's voice began to come through the radio. An electronics expert from the university swept the house and discovered a bugging device in the telephone connection box fixed to the wall of the house.

Joseph also alleges that although they lived in a minor street, police cars were frequently seen driving slowly past their home.

At the end of February his appeal against the convictions for assault, and for refusing to give a blood sample, was heard in the High Court. Justice Hansen's decision was reserved, and was released on 12 March 1997. In his judgement Justice Hansen noted in relation to the police witnesses:

I am extremely conscious of the advantage of the learned District Court Judge, as a Judge of first instance, seeing the witnesses and being able to observe them. This Court of

Appeal is loth to interfere with such findings of fact. But, in my view, the inconsistencies here were so great that it was not simply a matter where they could be so readily dismissed.

He then goes on to list examples of the major inconsistencies in the evidence of a police officer and others, and concludes his judgement with the following words:

From the above, it is apparent that there are significantly different accounts of the events of the evening, and I accept Mr Davis's [Joseph's lawyer] submission that both differing accounts do not deal with matters that are trite or insignificant. They deal with matters of real significance. Furthermore, they are most germane to the case for the defence, as advanced at trial. With all due respect to the learned District Court Judge, I have formed the view that those inconsistencies were not immaterial to the case.

For those reasons, I am satisfied that the appropriate course is to quash the conviction, and order a retrial on all three of the charges for which an appeal has been lodged.

After all Joseph's hundreds of hours and pages of letter writing, this was his first small taste of justice. But the strange occurrences that were happening showed no signs of abatement. On 14 March a mufti police car picked Joseph up as he was leaving the mosque, and stopped him for a breathalyser test. When that showed a negative result, he was accused of driving while disqualified, and issued with two traffic infringement notices. Joseph laid another complaint with the PCA, alleging harassment, intimidation, common assault by one of the officers, and fabrication of evidence. By this stage Joseph carried a mini recorder with him, and had a tape recording of the entire proceedings.

On 8 April, at 8.15 p.m., two police officers served a summons on him to appear in court on 21 May concerning the mufti car incident.

On 2 May, Joseph requested that the Attorney-General initiate criminal charges against the four policemen he alleged had beaten him up.

On 5 May he complained to the Crown Law Office that there had been no pre-arrest enquiries made into the allegations of sexual impropriety against him, as far as his alibis were concerned.

Joseph then became convinced of a plot to murder him involving, among others, two police officers. He continued to make complaints and allegations to the police, the Crown Law Office and the Police Complaints Authority.

On 16 July 1997, Joseph's retrial for the assault charges and the refusal to supply a blood sample was heard before Judge Callander. Although the charge of refusing to give blood was dismissed the two assault charges were upheld, but Joseph was fined only a token $100 on each charge. He appealed these convictions.

By this time the Josephs' lives were in complete disarray. They were seeing ghosts at every corner, they were frightened to use their telephone, and they were in fear of their lives. Inquiries were taking place on all sorts of fronts — phone bugs, police harassment, plots to murder. None of them has ever been upheld, although this does not necessarily mean they were without some substance. The truth is extremely hard to find, and I have never attempted to find the answers to all these questions.

It was at about this time that Lindy Forbes contacted me. Since I was spending considerable time in the South Island on work to complete our petition to the Governor-General on behalf of David Bain, I was able to spend some time with the Josephs. My main focus was on the sexual charges against John Joseph, which carried long jail sentences if he were found guilty, and the charge against Lindy of attempting to pervert the course of justice.

By this time Joseph had acquired, on legal aid, the services of Barrie Atkinson QC. I met Barrie to discuss the situation, and I also met with members of Joseph's support group. I analysed the evidence against him, as well as his alibis and other matters which he maintained confirmed his innocence. Both Joseph and Lindy maintained that he had never had any sexual contact with either of the two women, and that the charges were totally without foundation.

It was evident that Joseph was by now viewed with suspicion by the Christchurch police, and they would be determined to bring these charges to court.

My own position at the time was that Joseph himself, by his demeanour, attitude and appearance, was his own worst enemy. While he was undoubtedly extremely intelligent, at the same time he seemed to lack cultural sensitivity and understanding. He was sometimes belligerent in the manner in which he dealt with people, and came across as what we might call a 'bit of a smart-ass'.

I'm sure it was this aspect of his nature that caused the original rift between him and his father-in-law, and sparked the situation with the two police officers who stopped him and breath-tested him, the incident which it appeared to me set off the entire train of events that were to follow. Be that as it may, there were certain matters that I could not dismiss.

Dr Ron Macintyre, who had worked with Joseph at the university and was a member of his support group, told me that he called Joseph's in-laws in an attempt to settle the rift between them. He said that the father-in-law was vituperative in his denigration of Joseph.

One matter that seemed to me to be fundamental to the entire saga was to do with whether Joseph drank alcohol or not. Soon after meeting the Josephs and familiarising myself with the proceedings, I contacted a senior member of the Christchurch CIB who was involved in the case. He assured me that Joseph was not what he seemed. He was a drinker and a womaniser, the cop said. He advised me to stay clear of the whole situation and leave it to the cops who, he contended, were far better placed than I was to know the truth about Joseph.

And yet, no scrap of evidence has ever been produced by the police to show that Joseph has ever purchased or consumed alcohol. When he blew in the bag on that first night, it gave a negative result. Why, then, was he taken to the police station at all? From time to time he did, as his wife and associates were aware, visit bars and night clubs. His credit card receipts show that he spent very little money, and according to him he drank only orange juice.

It seemed to me that since he did not deny going to these places, and used a credit card to make his purchases, the police could easily obtain evidence from the bar staff or other people present that he was drinking alcohol, if in fact that was the case. I say this because if the police had been able to demonstrate that Joseph was lying when he stated that he never drank, because of his religion, then all Joseph's claims of innocence would have been destroyed.

So although on the one hand I was confronted with a man

whose attitude and demeanour did not serve his cause well, he also seemed from my dealings with him to be a man of honour and integrity, a belief that was supported by others who knew him well.

In addition, my readings of the evidence against him with regard to the sex charges, which were serious indeed and included two of rape, left me with a feeling of considerable unease.

First, the allegations had been made by two women of questionable reliability, some considerable time after the offences were alleged to have taken place. Second, the fact that both allegations were made at roughly the same time was also disturbing. It seemed an unlikely coincidence. And third, the timing of the complaints themselves, coinciding almost exactly with the court case involving the charges of assaulting two of the police officers, caused me concern. In addition, an examination of the statements made by the complainants contrasted with the charges actually made in an alarming manner.

Finally, the fact that Lindy knew each of these women quite well, yet did not believe a word they said, and was able to back up that belief with evidence as to her involvement and whereabouts at the time of the alleged incidents, which supported John's alibi, was the source of considerable disquiet.

I could not help but wonder whether somehow the strife Joseph found himself in with the police was not related to these apparently questionable complaints. I reflected on the circumstances of Dean Cottle, the defence witness who never got to give evidence in the Bain case. Cottle found himself in strife with the police, and was subsequently subjected to a barrage of criminal charges, all of which were either thrown out or not proven. Could this be a police tactic? I wondered.

By this time I had become aware of Bryan Rowe's successful

investigation into the Wicked Willies case. I rang Rowe and asked if he could assist the Josephs. Unfortunately he was too busy to take on the case, but he suggested another private investigator, Peter Hilt. I briefed Hilt, who took the assignment, and in addition I agreed to pay his fee. Hilt visited Christchurch, and conducted a detailed investigation into the situation. His enquiries caused him considerable concern, along much the same lines as my own. Some remarkable anomalies which were apparent to me were confirmed by Hilt.

One of the complainants, in statements made to the police in October and November, alleged that sexual misconduct by Joseph took place on 15 July, 2 August and 15 August 1996. Now the injuries Joseph sustained at Christchurch police station occurred on 14 June. One of these injuries was a broken ankle, as a result of which his leg was in a cast.

The allegations of this woman are bizarre to say the least. She alleges that Joseph brought condoms with him, and that she watched as he put them on. She says that he made her kneel on the floor on all fours and that he came up behind her, took his trousers off and had sex with her. This was the 2 August visit, and constituted one of the rape charges. On 15 August, she alleged, he again came to her flat, and ordered her to go into her bedroom and wait for him there. She says: 'He told me to go down on all fours, doggy style. Again I didn't resist as I knew he was angry.' He is then alleged to have had sex with her in this position and ejaculated twice.

She goes on to state that he then asked her to go into the shower, where he washed her, then put another condom on and had anal sex with her. All this allegedly happened within a matter of twenty minutes, at a time when John Joseph had his leg in plaster!

Remarkably, she says that on both these occasions he had phoned her and told her he was coming to visit her! Even more remarkable is the fact that although what is described as having taken place on 2 August is virtually identical to the events of 15 August, with the exception of the shower part, he was not charged with any offence in relation to the 15 August visit. Based on her statements, the police therefore believed that Joseph visited her on 2 August and raped her, yet she admitted him again after he had called her on 15 August, and he raped her again, but was not charged.

Another outstanding anomaly is that on 2 August, the date to which the rape charge applies, the woman took up her position on all fours, watched Joseph take down his trousers and put a condom on, then remained on all fours while he had his way with her.

Joseph for his part denied ever having any sexual contact with her at all. Prior to charges being laid, the police made no effort to clarify Joseph's whereabouts at the time of the alleged offences. Joseph posted notice of alibi. The police response to this was to take further statements from the complainant which had the effect of contradicting Joseph's claim that he was elsewhere at the time of the alleged incidents.

The second woman's complaints were not made until 25 November, and were alleged to have occurred on 30 March, some eight months earlier. This woman had a serious history of psychiatric problems, and had previously made many unfounded and unproven allegations against a variety of people, including close members of her family. Had it not been for the serious nature of the allegations, the situation would have been laughable.

Eventually the matter went before the Christchurch District Court and Judge C.J. Doherty in a jury trial on 15 June 1998.

Barrie Atkinson QC was Joseph's defence. The two complainants obtained name suppression and presented their evidence.

I attended a good part of the trial and was interested to note the presence of quite a number of staff from the team policing unit (those involved in the original alleged 'beating-up' incident), although they were not in any way involved in the proceedings. It seemed to make a mockery of the public perception that the police are short staffed when members of the force who are on duty can sit and observe a trial in which they have no official involvement.

The trial proceedings were acrimonious, and the cross-examination lengthy and destructive. There was a great deal of legal manoeuvring. Finally the trial turned into a fiasco and it became clear that the most serious rape charges were unlikely to be upheld. Suddenly, as the prosecution case drew to a close, looking pretty sick, the Crown announced that another woman who had read the daily press accounts of the trial had decided to make herself known to the police and lay further charges. Not only were these outrageous charges, in my opinion, they arose so opportunely that one could only view them with incredulity. However, according to the police they were serious, and would be proceeded with, unless . . . The next thing that happened came as a bombshell, and sent Joseph into fits of rage. It took several people to control him and calm him down.

Right at the point when the new complaint was laid on the table, the Crown sought leave to propose a deal to Joseph's counsel. This was what's called a plea bargain. I was with Barrie Atkinson and John Joseph in private chambers at the court when Atkinson put the deal to Joseph. The deal was that the Crown would drop the rape charges, and would not bring the new charge if Joseph would plead guilty to the two lesser charges. In addition, they would recommend that the charge against Joseph's wife, of perverting the course of justice, be dropped. They would also endorse a sentence at the lower end of the scale (a suspended sentence), bearing in mind that the two charges Joseph was being asked to plead guilty to were minor. The two serious rape charges carried a potential sentence of eight or ten years. The other two sexual misdemeanour charges, for a first offender, might attract no more than a fine or a suspended sentence.

In effect the Crown case had collapsed. After two years, involving thousands of hours and probably hundreds of thousands of dollars, the case had fallen to bits in the process of the trial. The reason was simply that the allegations of the two women were quite unbelievable and did not stand up to close examination.

John Joseph was beside himself with rage. On the one hand he found it morally and ethically unacceptable to take the stand and plead guilty to something he had not done. On the other hand, he realised that if he did not do this the Crown would throw the book at him and his wife. He risked an extremely lengthy jail term for himself and possibly one for his wife as well; this with two pre-school daughters to care for.

I will never forget watching John Joseph force himself to plead guilty to the two lesser charges, holding back the tears and knowing that he was innocent. If ever a moment symbolised the injustice that can occur in the criminal justice system in this country, this was it.

Joseph's counsel, Barrie Atkinson, was tempted to fight all the way, believing there was a good chance that Joseph would be acquitted on all charges, and that Lindy would escape the perversion of justice charge. But in the end he had to forgo his principles and accept the reality of the situation. It was obvious that there would be no respite for the Josephs until this matter was resolved. It seemed that the only sensible advice was to accept the plea bargain.

Astonishingly, this was still not the end of this incredible saga. The probation officer's report recommended either a fine or a suspended sentence if custodial sentence was considered appropriate. The Crown conceded that the offences were at the lower end of the scale and that a custodial sentence was not required. But the judge sentenced Joseph to twelve months' imprisonment!

Once again Atkinson appealed the sentences, which were reduced by the Court of Appeal. John Joseph was released from prison in late 1998. Within days he and his family returned to Egypt, where they are now settled and living a normal life.

Lindy's charge of attempting to pervert the course of justice was thrown out at a depositions hearing.

I have not bothered to find out what, if anything, has happened to the police officers involved in this case. Nor have I bothered to check the conclusions drawn by the PCA in relation to the complaints made to it by Joseph.

I conclude this account with John Joseph's final act in relation to his experience of the New Zealand criminal justice system. The following is the abbreviated text of a letter he wrote to the presiding judge on the day of his sentencing.

Dear Judge Doherty,

Your Honour was my trial judge from 15 to 18 June, during which I changed my plea to guilty in response to a 'plea bargain' and it was then the charges on counts 2 and 3 were dropped. You would have understandably been unaware of all the circumstances which have surrounded my family and I for two years since I was savagely beaten up by four police officers in Christchurch Central Police Station on 14 June 1996. However, I have provided the Probation Officer, Mr Kevin Harper, with a chronology and supporting reference letters that offer an insight to the irregular circumstances we have suffered at the hands of some members of the Christchurch Police Force. Unfortunately I had no chance whatsoever to explain to the court my case or defend myself whilst being misleadingly portrayed by a malicious prosecution.

... I thought it bad enough that from time to time innocent people are wrongfully convicted as with Arthur Allan Thomas, but I would never have thought the day would come when an innocent person like myself would be forced to plead guilty to a crime he has never committed.

It was under extreme duress and compulsion that I changed my plea from innocent to guilty. I came from Egypt with a strong legal background. Egypt is a country with more than 7000 years of civilisation which encapsulates a vast heritage of justice systems throughout history ... In our legal culture, a plea bargain is considered unethical and should the prosecutor believe the accused to be innocent then he would be under unequivocal moral obligation to drop the charge(s).

Whilst I do appreciate that we are not in Egypt, justice should always be about fairness, righteousness, factuality and proof, not about bargaining charges or convictions.

I felt pressured to change my plea to guilty for the following reasons:

1. I had to consider the future and safety of my family,

especially my wife who was facing a false charge of perverting the course of justice (which the Crown agreed to undertake a recommendation to the police that they urgently address dropping this charge if I pleaded guilty).

2. In addition I have been subject to numerous death threats and constant police harassment up to the very last day of my recent trial. It was imperative I consider not only my personal safety but that of my wife and two young daughters.

3. I was threatened that if I did not plead guilty I would face more charges on top of the rape charges which were punishable for 20 years.

4. When I was forced to plead guilty to one charge of indecent assault in relation to [the first complainant] both the police and prosecution agreed to drop the other charge in relation to [the second complainant] after obtaining her consent. Unfortunately they were unable to contact her and I was told that the court wanted to proceed with the case as a matter of urgency which put me under pressure as I was not given the luxury of having the case adjourned to the following morning, which would have enabled the police to reach the complainant and get her consent.

5. I was also told that if the trial continued I must plead guilty to the charge of the indecent assault of [the first complainant] in front of the jury. With all due respect, I felt my position would have been seriously compromised and I would have been prejudiced, which would have left me with little chance to receive an acquittal on the other charge if the jury saw me pleading guilty with regard to one complainant.

I sincerely feel that because I pleaded guilty under duress and compulsion, I will never forgive myself for comprom-ising my dignity and integrity and still steadfastly maintain my innocence, and if necessary I am willing to be put in the witness box to prove so. I would rather die and be killed with honour as an innocent person rather than live with the shame of having compromised myself by pleading guilty to crimes which I have never committed, and I therefore feel the only crime I am guilty of is the one towards myself when I changed my plea to guilty under such duress and compulsion as I have endeavoured to outline to you.

Chapter 13

In defence of the police

The system of justice as practised in Great Britain, the US, Canada, Australia, New Zealand and a number of British colonies and former colonies is what is known as the adversarial system. The foundation of this system is the presumption of innocence and the right to a fair trial for any person accused by the state of a crime.

Now in principle this is all very well. In practice, it has developed over many centuries into a courtroom drama that does not guarantee justice being done. In addition, the 'head in the sand' syndrome is nowhere more prevalent in society than in the minds of the practitioners of the justice system as we know it.

It is necessary at this point to draw a distinction between civil proceedings and criminal proceedings. For the most part, civil proceedings arise as a result of some degree of commercial risk on the part of those involved. A newspaper or some other publication, for example, wants to publish sensational stories to increase sales of its product. It therefore continually treads a fine line between sensationalism and truth, always aware of the risk of libel. The *Woman's Day* story on David Bain's life is a good example of this. The point is that in these circumstances the parties involved, although not necessarily equal in terms of financial clout or muscle, are generally both players in the game, and the 'injured' party ultimately has the *choice* of whether to pursue redress through the courts. David Bain, in the example quoted, could have chosen to let matters lie if he had so wished.

Similarly, when citizens have run-ins with government departments, for example the Inland Revenue Department, there are generally opportunities for discussion, negotiation and settlement. Redress through the courts can be sought as a final recourse.

In other words, while life is not always fair, we do have the opportunity to fight back. When we enter into business deals or commercial transactions that turn sour, we can seek legal redress if we wish.

This clearly is not the case in the criminal justice system, particularly in relation to serious crimes. On being charged with an offence, we are immediately apprehended and detained until the time of the trial. There are obvious reasons for this; where a serious crime has been committed and a criminal caught, it is logical to lock them up before they do it again or escape.

The second distinction between civil and criminal proceedings is based on the normal citizen's perception of what actually takes place in a court of law. This is largely based on sensational works of fiction, or television productions such as *Rumpole of the Bailey*, *Perry Mason* and more recently *Murder One*.

I think it can fairly be said that, almost without fail, most people's actual experience of court proceedings leaves them feeling bewildered, confused and disappointed. Anyone who has gone to a lawyer to discuss issuing civil proceedings will no doubt have been warned of 'the dangers of litigation'. In civil proceedings, however, there is a choice of whether to proceed, risks and all, or not. In criminal cases there is no such choice.

At the coalface of the New Zealand criminal justice system are the New Zealand Police, who are responsible for enforcing criminal law. In the District Court, summary offences are prosecuted by trained police officers. There are various sources of New Zealand law. Common law, sometimes referred to as case-made or judge-made law, is based on general principles or precedents developed over many centuries in England, and which became part of New Zealand law in 1840. Then there are New Zealand statutes; that is, those laws passed by Parliament. Statute law can reverse or amend common law. And in addition there are also a number of British statutes that are still in force in New Zealand.

The legal system is administered by a series of courts. The highest court in New Zealand is the Court of Appeal, under which are the High Court and then the District Court. At the head of the tribunals in New Zealand's legal system is the Judicial Committee of the Privy Council, which sits in London and is primarily made up of eminent British judges. It is more widely used in civil proceedings than criminal proceedings. Although controversial criminal cases continue to be appealed at the Privy Council, success is rare.

In addition to the courts there is one further avenue of appeal. This is the prerogative of mercy, or the power to grant pardons, which is vested in the Governor-General of New Zealand. The decree or issue of a royal pardon is not a remission based on a technicality or point of law. It is a statement of innocence. Section 407 of the Crimes Act of New Zealand states: 'The person so pardoned is deemed never to have committed the offence.'

When a case comes to trial, the integrity of the evidence is a critical factor in the game of justice, the game played out in the courtroom. In cases of injustice I have examined, the lack of integrity of the evidence has escaped detection by the jurists, and/or the jurors. It is at this point that I come to the defence of the police.

In recent years a number of books have been written which address the failings of the justice system in countries which share a similar system to New Zealand. One of the most interesting is an Australian book by Evan Whitton, which is entitled *The Cartel — Lawyers and Their Nine Magic Tricks*. Whitton has had an illustrious career as a journalist, writer and public commentator. He has been the editor of the *National Times*, chief reporter and European correspondent for the *Sydney Morning Herald*, reader in journalism at the University of Queensland, journalist of the year, five times winner of the Walkley award for national journalism, and is the author of four other books.

A highly acclaimed British publication is David Rose's 1996 book *In the Name of the Law — the Collapse of Criminal Justice*. The first two paragraphs of *In the Name of the Law* read:

> To destroy what was left of the old regime in criminal justice required just five words. They were uttered at the Old Bailey by the Lord Chief Justice of England at midday on the 19th of October 1989. The words were: 'The officers must have lied.'
>
> Lord Lane's comment on the Surrey police detectives who elicited confessions from the Guildford four exploded like a depth charge in a placid lake. His horror and cold fury were harbingers of tidal waves that have yet to subside.

In March 2000 another book that relates to this subject was published in the US. *Actual Innocence* was co-authored by Barry Scheck, Peter Newfeld and Jim Dwyer. Barry Scheck and Peter Newfeld founded and direct the Pro-bono Innocence Project at Benjamin N. Cardozo School of Law, which seeks the release of wrongly convicted people, largely, but not exclusively, through the use of DNA testing. They are both prominent civil rights attorneys in private practice in New York. Jim Dwyer is a novelist who has twice been awarded the Pulitzer Prize, and currently writes for the *New York Daily News*.

I am simply a citizen of one of the world's smallest Western countries, endowed with what we are continually told is one of the fairest police forces in the world, who four years ago saw a case of what I believe to be gross injustice, and has been fighting to right the wrong ever since. The conclusions I have reached during those four years are borne out by these highly qualified and dedicated commentators and lawyers in other parts of the world which have a criminal justice system closely resembling our own.

In earlier times, when criminals were far less sophisticated and crime less of an industry, before television thrust violence and criminal activity into the living room of every home in the developed world, the role of the police in society was significantly different to the role they are required to fill today. The 'copper' was seen as a stalwart of society, not particularly bright, perhaps, but solid and reliable. Offenders were apprehended and brought before the court. Simple, straightforward evidence was called.

Over time, defence lawyers who were unable to satisfactorily dismantle the evidence sought refuge in legal semantics to defend their clients. The role of the judge became less one of judgement, and more one of interpreting the law. They became arbiters in the battle between the two sides — the defence and the prosecution. As time went on more and more 'factually' guilty people were acquitted due to the cleverness of their defence lawyers in applying the law, using the devices that Evan Whitton calls 'the lawyer's nine magic tricks'.

Naturally, this incensed the policeman who, while risking life and limb to keep the peace and make arrests, developed a feeling of futility at the outcome of the proceedings. The inevitable result of this was that the prosecution had to become more inventive to secure convictions. Gradually, over many decades, even centuries, the courtroom evolved into a forum where protagonists took as much liberty with the truth as possible in order to win. Winning became the sole objective. Winners became famous, increased their social status, and advanced through the ranks.

When winning becomes the sole objective in any situation, the human factor plays an ever-increasing role. Short cuts are taken, tricks are played. As in sport, people cheat to win, unless or until they are found out. And so criminal justice has been reduced to a game of win or lose. The goal is no longer to discover the truth, but simply to win. And without truth there can be no justice.

In defence of the police, I say only this. The manner in which the application of criminal justice has evolved over the centuries has meant that unconsciously the police have developed a culture which has led to the acceptance of a culture of 'noble corruption', which is another way of saying that the end justifies the means. The theory goes something like this: the copper is sure he has caught the culprit. The culprit is a threat to society (the copper believes); he needs to be put away. The evidence is a bit skinny so the copper beefs it up a bit (or a lot), thereby, he believes, doing society a favour. Noble indeed.

But it does not take much imagination to see how that attitude can lead to far worse applications of the principle by ambitious, lazy or prejudiced individuals. In my opinion this is the thin end of the wedge, which has seen the entire process of criminal justice develop into a charade. It has resulted in the collapse of the criminal justice system in Western countries, to the point where in Great Britain, Australia and the US police corruption is endemic, professional criminals have an 80 percent chance of permanently escaping detection, and the many poor innocents who have fallen victim to this collapse are being marched off to prison.

The August 1999 edition of the US Department of Justice *Law Enforcement Bulletin* contains an article entitled 'Noble Cause Corruption and the Police Ethic', written by Chief Bob Harrison, who leads the Vacaville Police Department in California. Harrison invites the reader to consider the question, 'Does an officer have the duty to infringe on an individual's liberty for a laudable outcome?' He also poses the question, 'How can police officers maintain an appropriate balance between governing others and controlling themselves?' He answers these questions himself in this way:

> When officers use unlawful means to gain a desired end they damage the system they represent. Beyond the damage to the justice system, however, illegal behaviour denigrates not only the uniform of the guardian but also the individual within. The eventual result to society is a loss of confidence in those charged with the protection of others, leading to a fraying of the tapestry of the culture that binds communities together . . . Once equality and confidence in the institution of policing is eroded in the general community, the ability for government to fulfil its legitimate aims also becomes decimated.

He states that confidence in police courtroom testimony is

severely eroded in the United States, and says, 'For example, in one East Coast city the term "testilying" is a code word for police perjury to obtain a conviction.'

In opening his dissertation Harrison refers, as I have done, to the grand forefather of justice, Socrates. He states, 'In Plato's *The Republic* Socrates discusses the formation of a city that embodies justice', and he quotes, 'The city's guardians must be gentle toward their own people but rough toward their enemies; otherwise, they will not wait for others to destroy them: they will do it themselves first.'

* * *

In the book *Actual Innocence*, the stories are recounted of a number of cases in which the authors proved the innocence, and obtained the acquittal, of American citizens incarcerated for life, or in some cases on death row, by using DNA testing.

The inside front cover of the book reads:

A nightmare from a thousand B-movies: a horrible crime is committed in your neighbourhood, and the police knock at your door. A witness swears you are the perpetrator; you have no alibi and no one believes your protestations of innocence. You're convicted, sentenced to hard time in maximum security, or worse still on death row.

Tragically, this is no movie script but reality for hundreds of American citizens. Our criminal justice system is broken and people from all walks of life have been destroyed by its failures.

In the last ten years, DNA testing has uncovered stone cold proof that sixty-five people, completely innocent, have been sent to prison and death. But even in cases where there is physical evidence [of innocence] the criminal justice system frees prisoners only after a tortuous legal process. Incredibly, according to many trial judges, 'actual innocence' is not grounds for release from prison.

We cannot afford to take the stance that such things only happen in other countries. The point of considering international experience is to draw appropriate analogies and provide ways of reforming our own system.

The Janine Law case clearly demonstrates that our police are not infallible. If the police can be mistaken in such a straightforward case as this, and worse still cling doggedly to their inaccurate theory for five years, it seems obvious that this would not be an isolated case.

One paragraph in *Actual Innocence* summarises the manner in which false allegations of guilt brought about the ultimate conviction of innocent people:

In 1999 the Innocence Project reconstructed 62 of the 67 exonerations in North America to determine what factors had been prevalent in the wrongful convictions. They were:

Mistaken eye witnesses: 84%

Snitches or informants: 21%

False confessions: 24%

Defence lawyers fell down on the job: 27%

Prosecutorial misconduct: 50%

Defective or fraudulent science: 30%

The authors of *Actual Innocence* maintain that these numbers provide but a glimpse of an unexplored, undocumented and challenging world. Every state could use an innocence commission — none has one. Only the criminal justice system exempts itself from self-examination — wrongful convictions are seen not as catastrophes, but as topics to be avoided.

The authors go on to further analyse the reasons why the innocent were found guilty. Under the heading prosecutorial misconduct:

Suppression of exculpatory evidence: 43%
Coerced witnesses: 13%
False statements to jury: 8%
Evidence fabrication: 3%
Improper closing arguments: 8%
Knowing use of false testimony: 22%

Under the heading police misconduct:

Allegation of undue suggestiveness in pre-trial procedures: 33%
Coerced confession: 9%
Suppression of exculpatory evidence: 36%
Evidence fabrication: 9%

In relation to scientific work:

DNA inclusions: 1 case
Blood typing errors: 32 cases
Fingerprints and other physical evidence: 5 cases
Defective or fraudulent science: 21 cases
Microscopic hair comparison: 18 cases

While it would be wrong to conclude that identical patterns would emerge if cases of the innocent proven guilty in New Zealand were examined, the study is nevertheless worth considering since this is the only study of its type that has been carried out anywhere in the world at the present time. As the authors comment, in nearly every case where false guilt is exposed, the system does its best to sweep it out of the way and put it in the 'topics not to be talked about' file.

However, if we dare to examine the few identifiable cases in New Zealand, we do find some alarming similarities.

In late 1999 the family of Arthur Allan Thomas erected a memorial at the Thomas farm south of Pukekohe. This is the farm where Arthur was living at the time of his arrest. The Thomas family invited me to attend, and I found it a very moving occasion. The speakers included Jim Sprott, Pat Vesey, and old Mr Thomas, now 92 years old. Arthur's brothers and sister spoke with great sincerity, and very movingly. Thirty years on, these people have not forgotten.

They issued a leaflet as a keepsake to those who attended, and under one heading they had made a list. It read:

WHAT GOT ARTHUR THOMAS WRONGLY CONVICTED
Police — desperate for a conviction
    — ignored alibis
    — committed perjury
    — planted evidence
    — concealed and withheld evidence from the defence
    — stole crucial evidence
    — switched shellcase evidence in court
    — pressured witnesses
    — collaborated to pre-select jury

- used false evidence knowing it to be wrong
- dumped tampered evidence to avoid discovery of mischief
- warned off defence witnesses

If the list is categorised in the same way as the case studies in *Actual Innocence*, it is found to incorporate many of the same elements. And many of the same features can be found in the submission before the Governor-General in the case of David Bain. Categories that can be safely included are:

Defective scientific evidence
Non-disclosure of exculpatory evidence
Incorrect closing arguments
Use of false testimony (whether knowingly or unknowingly)
Deficiencies in the defence

Another aspect of the Innocence Project that shows a striking similarity to conditions in New Zealand is the absolute refusal of authorities to admit that an injustice has been done and act quickly to put it right, even in the face of overwhelming evidence.

For the most part the Innocence Project has more difficulty getting cooperation from authorities than it does in gathering proof of innocence. At least the project has an official base, the Cardozo School of Law in New York, and it now has the support of two states which have officially endorsed and authorised post-conviction DNA testing. Both Illinois and New York allow testing at any time if there is a reasonable possibility the tests will exonerate the inmate; they will even pay for it if the convicted person cannot afford to do so.

It is no surprise that of the 62 exonerations, a disproportionate number — 21 — come from these two states. In most other states the project has met with all the same obstacles that confront those fighting injustices in the criminal justice system in this country. In one classic pronouncement, a judge stated that 'a claim of actual innocence is not itself a constitutional claim'! In other words if a person is found guilty, having been through the due process of trials and appeals, then it is just hard luck if he or she is in fact innocent. I fear his words echo a sentiment commonly found in the upper echelons of the legalists of this country.

In the US, approximately six thousand people have been sent to death row since 1976, and about eighty of those have been acquitted for a variety of reasons. Many people in judicial circles in the US and, I would suggest, in New Zealand, believe that an error rate of one percent in the trial process for serious crimes is acceptable. What I find alarming is that in New Zealand, at least, in many of the contentious cases where the convicted protest their innocence, the evidence is often circumstantial and does not stand up to post-trial scrutiny. I find this alarming because it is with this type of evidence that the opportunity presents itself for the Crown to make extravagant claims in relation to what are absolutely innocent matters; for example, David Bain's fingerprints on the rifle. Also of concern is that so many convictions obtained by the Crown in serious crimes which are contentious rely very much on this type of evidence, that is, evidence which requires inferences or is capable of bearing several interpretations. Good examples of such cases are Barlow, Dougherty and obviously, Bain. So it is my belief that in serious crimes in this country the error rate may in fact be significantly higher than one per cent.

The authors of *Actual Innocence* have more individual and collective experience in why and how the system fails than anyone else in the world. The reason for this is that no official or unofficial study has been made by any justice system into how the innocent get convicted and what can be done about it.

My experience over the last four years leaves me in no doubt that when the barriers are finally broken in this country the similarities to the American experience will be striking.

* * *

In the Name of the Law — the Collapse of Criminal Justice, David Rose's analysis of criminal justice as it applies in Great Britain, is a less sensational and more clinical work than *Actual Innocence*. The British analogy is probably more pertinent to New Zealand than the American, as our system is almost a replica of the British system, and many British traditions and customs form the basis of our system.

Rose's fundamental theme is that the criminal justice system is in disarray, that it is hopelessly inadequate in apprehending and gaining convictions against real criminals, and at the same time has been and still is very prone to the false conviction of the innocent. I would suggest that the situation in New Zealand is very similar.

Rose writes that in England the 'contemporary crisis in criminal justice is not simply a matter of increasing demands on the system, although they have exacerbated it. The system is failing in its first and most essential task: to separate "factually guilty" criminals from the falsely accused.'

I would suggest again that exactly the same conclusion is valid in New Zealand.

A system that allows the state to send innocent people to jail but cannot be relied upon to bring offenders to justice is failing itself and those it represents. If this is the situation in New Zealand, then our justice system falls far short of meeting the responsibilities for which it exists in the first place.

Chapter 14

The collapse of the criminal justice system

It is the forlorn cry of many in our justice system 'that it is preferable for ten guilty men to go free than for one innocent one to be convicted'. This seems a hopelessly inadequate conscience-salving delusion. While a false fabric of guilt is an ever-increasing spectre confronting the innocent, the corollary is that a life of undisturbed criminal activity awaits those who pursue the path of crime.

The criminal justice system is failing on almost every front. The police are failing to stem the rising tide of criminal activity. When suspects who 'know the ropes' are brought before the courts, they stand a real chance of using the legalese and gamesmanship that characterise the adversarial system and walking free. That is, of course, if they are apprehended in the first place. On the other hand, being in the wrong place at the wrong time leaves the naive and unaware fully exposed to the vagaries of the same system.

I consider that complaints about the police to the PCA are a waste of time. The court system is a mockery as far as getting to the truth is concerned, and the appeal procedures are antiquated, unwieldy and self-defeating as a means of examining miscarriages of justice.

The role of the police

We know as a matter of fact that vast amounts of serious crime not only remain unsolved, but are not even seriously investigated. This relates particularly to crimes against property, where something like 90 percent of reported crimes remain unsolved. On the other hand, the police put incredible efforts into seeking retribution for crimes of a personal nature, such as domestic sexual abuse, and crimes which result in extensive media coverage and public interest.

The fundamental issue of whether or not the police have sufficient resources to maintain law and order has become a political football, with politicians manipulating the statistics to suit their particular perspective. To put it simply, politicians have nothing to gain by confronting the fact that the police are anything less than a noble organisation which stands alone as the barricade between society and the onslaught of crime. The recent removal from office of the police commissioner himself would not have occurred but for the incoming government's election promises in relation to the accountability of government administrators.

The police have been, and remain, accountable to nobody but themselves. The Minister of Police almost invariably supports the police whenever an allegation is made against them, as do associated ministers such as the Attorney-General and the Minister of Justice.

The simple fact is that votes are far more winnable on a 'fight against crime' platform than on one that espouses the idea of a clinical assessment of the effectiveness of the justice system, and the integrity of those responsible for its administration.

As for the judiciary, it seems so steeped in the tradition of accepting the integrity of the police that any reference to the contrary is treated with suspicion.

Because the police are such a law unto themselves, it is well nigh impossible to expose them when the situation demands, and so unacceptable procedures go undetected, becoming self-perpetuating to the point where they could now be said to be endemic. A good example of this relates to disclosure.

Until quite recently in our history, the right of full disclosure of evidence to the accused did not exist. It seems that since the Bill of Rights established this requirement as mandatory, the police have struggled to comply with it. Whenever failures of this type occur (such as the apparently destroyed statement in the Wicked Willies case) they are attributed to an unfortunate over-sight. My own experience has led me to believe that this type of occurrence is commonplace, and has proliferated as a result of political and judicial lack of interest.

It is vital that the agency responsible for proper disclosure carries out this responsibility with integrity, since they may well be the only agency that knows of the existence of relevant material. For example, if defence counsel is unaware that a particular interview was conducted by a policeman, he or she is not in a position to request copies of the notes of that interview. I realise that this is an almost asinine statement of the obvious, or as a now infamous American CEO once put it, 'a blinding glimpse of the obvious', known by his subordinates as a 'BGO'.

But the point must be made that it is so often the obvious that is overlooked, and in the complex fabric of legalese under which our justice system labours, the obvious is that truth and justice are inseparable concepts. Moreover, truth depends on openness, honesty and transparency. It is surely from this fundamental precept that the principle of disclosure is derived. But disclosure procedures are not simple, nor are there any real rules. In addition, the police seem to view disclosure as counterproductive to their interests, which inevitably raises the question of why they should hold such a view.

I believe it all relates back to the elementary reason for the failure of so many police investigations, which is their propensity to make up their minds too early, and then to ignore or discard any evidence contrary to that predetermined view. The Janine Law case, the Wicked Willies case and the David Bain case are but three examples which I believe graphically illustrate this point. It seems more than coincidental to me that so often what is not disclosed is probative of a contrary view, and thus perverts the whole process of justice from the outset.

It is worth recalling the opening of David Rose's *In the Name of the Law* to exemplify the point. When the Lord Chief Justice of England uttered the words, 'The officers must have lied', Rose states, 'Lord Lane's comment on the Surrey police detectives . . . exploded like a depth charge in a placid lake. His horror and cold fury were harbingers of tidal waves that have yet to subside.'

Is non-disclosure of relevant material any less a lie than a fabricated confession? Is a positive lie any less a lie than a negative one? What is the meaning of the oath taken by all witnesses in a court of law, to 'tell the whole truth and nothing but the truth'? It is a further BGO that a statement may be entirely true in itself and yet does not tell the actual truth.

If simple but broad standards for disclosure were set down for the police and other Crown agencies, then it seems to me that accountability must ensue. Failure to comply should automatic-ally result in the declaration of a mistrial, and such occurrences could be examined by a truly independent body (along the lines of the Serious Fraud Office) who would have the authority to recommend that the Crown institute criminal proceedings if this was deemed appropriate.

The so-called 'luminol' photographs in the David Bain trial are a prime example of non-disclosure of evidence and the significant effects this can have. Discussion of these photographs is included in Part I, chapter 7. Briefly, at the trial Detective Sergeant Weir gave evidence that luminol tests revealed five bloody footprints, which were measured and from their size adduced to be David's prints. They were particularly incriminating since they were found in an area where David said he had not been. When the detective was asked whether photographs of these footprints had been taken, he replied that the police photographer had taken photos of them, but they had not come out. The police photographer did not give evidence at the trial, so he could not be questioned about these photographs.

In the course of the police/PCA inquiry into the 'allegations' in *David and Goliath*, the police consulted a photographic expert, Peter Durrant, whose findings were then dismissed in the subsequent report. As a result I contacted Durrant, and in the course of our discussion he mentioned that the police had supplied him with two boxes of photographs of luminol footprints, each containing either 16 or 32 photographs! I eventually managed to persuade the police to let me examine these photographs, and found, perhaps not surprisingly, that what they depicted bore absolutely no resemblance to a footprint!

Several interesting points arise out of this. First, the police photographer did not give evidence at the trial so could not be questioned about the photographs. Second, when Weir stated that the photographs did not come out, was that a true statement? Had he been told they had not come out, or was there some other reason for his saying they had not come out?

The third interesting point, which is particularly relevant to the discussion on disclosure of evidence, was that David Bain's counsel did not know of the existence of these photographs, and they were not included in the material disclosed to him. The police may argue that had he requested a meeting with the police photographer, he would have discovered the photographs for himself. My view is that had proper procedures been in place, whereby all parties knew specifically what was required of them, and who was accountable, then this situation would have been much less likely to arise.

Disclosure is only one area in which court hearings can be subverted from the outset by the police. Suffice to say that it is incumbent on the police to investigate in a full and thorough manner, not to simply gather the evidence necessary to sustain a case against a person they believe to be the culprit.

Returning to the American situation recounted in *Actual Innocence*, while it has been the subsequent availability of DNA testing that has proven the innocence of the cases they have taken on, in almost every case deficient investigatory procedures can, with the benefit of hindsight, be blamed for the initial miscarriage of justice. In the view of the authors, when these deficiencies lead to the false accusation of guilt, they necessarily need to be bolstered by further obfuscation, which inevitably takes the form of defective science, prosecutorial complicity, misleading evidence or, even worse, false evidence by prosecution witnesses including the police themselves, and false confessions accepted in the face of contrary evidence.

The investigators, in other words the police, need to be scrupulously professional and meticulous in their assemblage of evidence. Until they can be certain of the truth, charges should not be laid.

It is for these reasons that I have formed the opinion that in the modern climate, where the media and public are so demanding, the role of the police in serious crime investigations requires a fundamental refocus. I would like to see a far more inquisitorial approach to criminal investigation, where discretion as to the direction of the inquiry is removed from the judgement of the police themselves. The police could then aggressively investigate without the burden of public expectation and peer pressure to make an arrest and effect a conclusion to a case.

For it is not difficult, if one thinks about it, to understand how an apparently compelling case can be made against a suspect who is entirely innocent. The rape conviction of David Dougherty in Auckland is a classic example of this, and exactly mirrors the American experiences of the Innocence Project.

In October 1992, an eleven-year-old girl was abducted from her home and raped. She claimed that Dougherty was her attacker. He maintained his innocence and gave a DNA sample to prove it. One must remember that DNA testing for forensic purposes was in its infancy at that time, and the tests were far less definitive than those that have been developed since.

In June 1993, Dougherty was convicted of rape and sentenced to an eight-year jail sentence. The girl's evidence was compelling and highly emotive. Dougherty's only alibi was his wife, who was not an effective witness. The DNA evidence at that trial was inconclusive; the tests that were available could not satisfactorily analyse the semen samples taken from the complainant's underwear.

In November 1993 David Dougherty's defence sought to have further, more sophisticated testing done by the ESR. These tests identified another man's semen in the girl's underwear, but the

ESR claimed that at the same time it found traces of Dougherty's DNA. On the strength of these findings Dougherty's case was taken to the Court of Appeal in October 1994, two years after the rape occurred. The Court of Appeal was not convinced by the latest DNA results and turned down the appeal.

It was at this time that Dr Arie Geursen became involved. He had read reports of the interpretation of this evidence at the Court of Appeal hearing, and as a result felt considerable unease. Now although Dr Geursen is a genetic physicist, at the time he had had nothing to do with David Dougherty, his family or his lawyers. He was simply not satisfied, due to his own knowledge and expertise, 'that the slant put on the DNA test results at the Court of Appeal were, on the face of it, correct'. He asked if he could examine the file, and this examination confirmed his suspicions.

At about this time Murray Gibson took over as Dougherty's lawyer. The new defence team set about re-examining the case against Dougherty, in particular the DNA evidence. The test results and source data were obtained from the ESR, and sent for review by two overseas experts, Dr Stephen Gutowski of the Victoria Forensic Science Centre, and Dr Rebecca Reynolds, who was involved in the actual development of the DNA test kit and procedure itself. Both these scientists agreed with Arie Geursen. They said that the tests show unequivocal evidence of another man's semen, and that the faint signals which the ESR claimed matched Dougherty's were in all probability an accidental cross-reaction in the test kit.

Murray Gibson petitioned the Governor-General in April 1996, and this petition was successful. On the Governor-General's advice, the case was referred back to the Court of Appeal in August 1996. This time, on the strength of the opinions of the overseas scientists, and that of Dr Geursen, Dougherty's conviction was quashed, he was released from jail, and a new trial was ordered.

The new trial took place in April 1997 at the High Court in Auckland. After ten hours of deliberation, the jury found Dougherty innocent and acquitted him on both charges — abduction and rape.

This is a case where both the High Court and the Court of Appeal had processed Dougherty's case and endorsed his guilt. A case which was 'proven beyond any reasonable doubt', in other words. And yet, when all the evidence was properly examined, and then retested before a further jury, his conviction was overturned.

David Dougherty can thank his lucky stars for two things: the intervention of a layperson, Arie Geursen, and the definitiveness of DNA evidence. It is most unusual for anyone from within the system to put right miscarriages of justice. Those 'in the system', be they scientists, judges, lawyers or police officers, are usually quite content to rely on the technical appearance of justice as delivered by due process. Arie Geursen was not. Something was wrong, and fortunately, in this case science was ultimately able to put it right.

It should be said that in this case it was not the police who directly contributed to the miscarriage of justice. It was faulty science that led to the conviction, and but for that faulty science, Dougherty would have been excluded from the outset.

While I do not have detailed knowledge of the original investigation, arrest and trial of David Dougherty, it is public knowledge that a police review of the case has confirmed that the police now believe Dougherty to be totally free of any suspicion or involvement in the original abduction and rape.

It seems to me that the point about professionalism and scrupulous analysis in the initial investigation is made even more clearly in this case. Although as I say the police are not held by any of the parties to have been primarily to blame for the false fabric of guilt that was to enmesh David Dougherty, they could, one must presume, have prevented it. But, in the political climate in which we live, an eleven-year-old girl who claims to have been raped, and in addition claims to be able to identify the rapist, is not to be disbelieved!

How much objectivity were her claims subjected to? What was the corroborating evidence, if any? Was there a motive or predisposition? Did her account of events tally with the facts in all regards, or did it need tailoring to eliminate loopholes? How strong was the scientific evidence? Were there other possible explanations? We don't have the answers to these questions, but quite clearly it is now accepted even by the police that the original investigators did 'get it wrong'.

Without the benefit of conclusive DNA tests, Dougherty would surely have served his eight-year sentence, and been forever tarnished by his conviction. Other cases, including David Bain, Peter Ellis, John Barlow and Rex Haig, all have a huge cloud of doubt hanging over them, but do not have the benefit of one simple test which, properly executed, could conclusively lead to the truth.

It seems to me that in cases where the evidence is circum-stantial or conflicting, where no compelling motive or mental precondition exists, or where science can be exhaustively processed to arrive at what seems like a certainty, the police must be ever alert to all possibilities and eliminate all doubt before taking the step of making an arrest. For, as we have seen in other cases, once that step is taken, a point of no return is reached.

In summary, what on the face of it is, to use the legal terminology, a 'prima facie' case, which seems strong, compelling and winnable in the courts, is not always factually the case at all.

The Bain case is a classic example in this regard. Almost all the exhaustive collection of evidence took place *after* David was arrested! At the time of his arrest he was adamant that he was innocent. There was no motive or mental predisposition. There was no trigger or precipitator. No blood testing of any description had been done. Ballistics tests had not been commenced. Key eyewitnesses had not been interviewed. Reconstructions had not been done. Alternative scenarios were obvious but had not been followed up.

As our petition to the Governor-General on David's behalf demonstrates, had these matters been attended to before an arrest was made, then in all likelihood a sustainable case against him would never have resulted.

By their very nature our trials are adversarial, and as a result they are not conducive to the discovery of truth — factual truth, that is. Because of this I believe that in the event that a person is wrongly charged in the first place, there is a very significant chance that the wrong will be compounded and endorsed by the adversarial trial that follows.

Before a case goes to trial in New Zealand, a pre-trial hearing called a depositions hearing takes place. In the past these hearings would be presided over by a magistrate, now known as a district court judge. In recent times, however, in order it seems to free up judges and save money, depositions are almost exclusively presided over by justices of the peace.

The purpose of a depositions hearing is for the Crown to 'depose' its evidence, or in more common parlance to present the evidence against the accused to confirm that a 'prima facie' case exists. Put another way, depositions hearings are to establish that the Crown has a case worthy of prosecution. The accused's lawyer is at liberty to cross-examine witnesses, and can call evidence on their client's behalf, although this seldom occurs.

Supporters of the current system may argue that depositions are the test of objectivity that the system provides, and that they ensure that only worthy cases go before the courts for a full trial. The defence has the opportunity of cross-examining Crown witnesses, thereby testing their veracity and credibility, and of calling evidence of its own if it so desires. This, it could be argued, gives the accused ample opportunity to expose a case of wrongful accusation.

Paradoxically, I would suggest that as a general rule it has the opposite effect, as does the later trial process. I believe it is of assistance to the 'factually guilty', and disadvantageous to the 'factually innocent'!

Let me explain. The factually guilty can set about fabricating a defence against the evidence put up, based on creating doubt in the jury's mind. They use what Evan Whitton calls the 'lawyers' nine magic tricks' to undermine the Crown case, which has been laid out before them at the depositions hearing. On the other hand, the factually innocent, lacking the benefit of a proper investigation (otherwise they would never have been charged), is stuck with trying to prove their innocence in a negative way. What I mean by this is that if the police have not followed up on avenues of investigation probative of the accused's innocence, then evidence in the accused's favour is not available to their defence.

A good example of this is the case of Scott Watson, who was convicted of murdering Ben Smart and Olivia Hope. This discussion is not about whether Watson is guilty or not; I am simply raising a matter to illustrate my point. It will be recalled that during the investigation into the disappearance of Ben Smart and Olivia Hope, a number of eyewitnesses stated that the two victims and the mystery man were dropped off by the water taxi in the early hours of New Year's Day at a two-masted ketch, with portholes down the side, and a bevy of ropes hanging over the back. This is quite different in appearance to Watson's single-masted sloop, which is much smaller, has one mast, no portholes and no ropes.

The Crown evidence was that no such ketch existed, that all the eyewitnesses who said they saw the ketch were either mistaken or presumably lying. It may be argued that the jury had the benefit of hearing from these witnesses, and clearly decided that they were either mistaken or lying, or that even if they were correct it did not matter in the case against Watson. But just for the sake of argument, let's assume that it was a ketch at which they were dropped off. It would be almost impossible, months after the event, and without the resources of the police, for the defence to find that ketch.

In other words, and speaking in general terms, if the police inquiry at the time of a crime fails to find, or ignores (for whatever reason), significant evidence, it is highly unlikely that a defence team months, or sometimes years, later will be able to uncover it. My point is that the factually innocent are more severely disadvantaged, as the only evidence available is against them, and the evidence that could prove their innocence is either lost with the passage of time and/or unavailable due to a lack of resources.

The Wicked Willies case is particularly germane to this point. Had the accused in that case been unable to afford the services of Bryan Rowe they would probably have gone down, since the only evidence available would have been the false and contaminated evidence called by the Crown. They were extremely fortunate that the evidence available to prove their innocence could be elucidated at all. So often, once police inquiries have been completed the people available as witnesses are loth to come forward, due to an instinctive fear of complicating their lives.

Before leaving the subject of faulty and inadequate police investigations, it is salient to recall the case of the five Gisborne police officers who faced 24 serious allegations involving corruption of the worst kind: aggravated robbery, supply of drugs, theft of drugs and obstructing the course of justice.

Anyone interested in the mechanisms of police investigations would do well to read the account of this saga by award-winning *New Zealand Herald* journalist Miriyana Alexander, contained in her book *Presumed Guilty*, which was published in 1998.

In this case the entire set of charges against all the officers was thrown out at the depositions hearing! This leads to a number of serious conclusions, all of which are relevant to the points I have been making.

Firstly, the New Zealand Police Association came to the defence of the officers under investigation, and funded their defence. I believe they spent in excess of $200,000 on legal costs and hiring private investigators. Normal members of the public seldom have such resources at their disposal. Without the funding, these officers would have been in deep mire.

Secondly, the accused themselves, being police officers, know how the system works and, in particular, know how police inquiries are conducted, and so were quite capable of defending themselves.

Thirdly, as a result of these two factors the defence was able to mount an attack on the 'so-called' evidence against them at the depositions hearing — an almost unheard of course of action — and the charges were rejected. Had the charges been defended in a criminal trial, they would have been much more difficult to overcome, due to the adversarial nature of the system under which our trials are conducted.

Let me give an insight into what everyone except Commissioner Peter Doone thought of what had taken place, by borrowing a few quotes from Miriyana Alexander's book. The Gisborne Police Association Chairman, Sergeant Paul Stuart, is quoted quite extensively, but I shall restrict my examples to those most relevant in this context.

'We fully accept that there had to be an inquiry. However, we believe the inquiry team involved in this investigation became quickly subjective instead of remaining objective,' he said.

'As professional police officers we are trained to ensure a person is accorded the basic rights outlined in the Bill of Rights. Yet some of our members feel they were not afforded these rights.

'[Our] belief and loyalty no longer extends to the senior administration of the New Zealand Police, with whom they have lost all faith.'

Following the dismissal of all charges, Judge Russell Callander was appointed to investigate the fiasco. His initial report raised eyebrows at police national headquarters, and he ended up 'watering down' (Alexander's words) his remarks.

A second version was produced three months later, and the Hamilton police officers who conducted the investigation were deeply upset by its comments. They were given the opportunity to reply, but despite that, the final report came out largely unchanged from the second 'watered down' version.

Basically the judge made three telling findings:

a. the investigating team formed a mindset that the accused were guilty;
b. many available and potential witnesses had not been interviewed [no doubt due to the fact that they would not support the mindset already arrived at];
c. proper prosecution criteria were not met in making the decision to lay charges.

Does this not mirror many of the other examples I have referred to in this book, and exemplify the 'noble justice' concept of:

a. a mindset that someone is guilty;
b. ignoring any evidence or available evidence to the contrary; and
c. pressing on with the prosecution process by laying charges anyway?

Judge Callander went on to make some very damning remarks, which are highly pertinent to my own argument. He said:

> To be selective in who is interviewed is to invite a charge of bias. It was evidence later gleaned from these witnesses [by the private investigator hired by the accused officers] that enabled defence counsel . . . to highlight the already evident credibility problems and cripple the prosecution cases.
>
> . . . When charges are laid, loyalty lines are drawn. This is one of the defects of the adversarial system.

On the issue of mindset, Judge Callander states:

Difficult police cases are often only solved because detectives are persistent and single-minded. A subtle shift from the single-minded to the set-minded may be unintended and unconscious.

And on the issue of police investigating other police officers:

Experience here and overseas shows that the investigation into alleged police misconduct is not only inordinately difficult, but usually satisfies no one.

As an American police internal affairs officer explains it, 'officers think we're out to get them, and the public think we're out to cover up for them'.

On the issue of the decision to lay charges, the judge's comments are salient not just to this particular case, but to every single case, and particularly relevant to my beliefs. His comments are forthright, far-reaching and go to the very core of many of the problems I have attempted to highlight in this book. He states:

The decision to charge is the single most important decision made in the course of criminal proceedings. It lies at the very core of a system of justice.

Once the decision to charge has been made, the storm begins: irreversible tides will engulf the main players, changing their lives forever.

The fear and consequences (media scrutiny, personal distress, family tension, financial burden) of criminal court proceedings and their outcomes are profound. An eventual dismissal of the case is no consolation to an accused person.

Another of his points relates to guidelines for prosecutions:

> The provision [that prosecutions should proceed even when there is doubt] essentially passes the buck to the court. If there is doubt, then the position is clear, there should be no prosecution.

Finally, the judge stated that Crown solicitors should be given the right to discontinue proceedings. While at the time of charging a reasonable prospect of conviction might seem likely, he said, the situation could change as the case was being prepared. 'In such a case, the prosecutor should have the power to discontinue.'

The judge also recommended that some Australian and Canadian prosecution practices be adopted. In particular, he noted Australian guidelines on determining the credibility of witnesses, and the Canadian practice of getting a senior, independent Queen's Counsel to decide, in sensitive public issue cases, whether a prosecution was necessary, and had merit.

The barrister for the accused officers, John Haigh QC, is quoted in *Presumed Guilty* as saying:

> If this case leads to a review of the prosecution process not just for police officers but for everyone, then something will have been achieved.

The decision to prosecute is critical. The wrong decision was made in this case, and it's time that process was overhauled.

I conclude with one last comment from Judge Callander's review, which echoes the entire sentiments of this work, and the sentiments and beliefs that have driven me so powerfully over the past four and a half years. The italics are mine:

It is hoped that lessons have been learnt from this review. A police force of integrity is crucial to our democracy: *without such the rule of law becomes but a meaningless phrase.*

Who watches the watchdog?

In the final analysis, the police/PCA review into what had been called at its inception the 'unfounded allegations' in *David and Goliath* was flawed at a fundamental level. If Colin and I had not been able to convince the PCA at the meeting of 25 July to reopen certain matters, the result would have been even more shameful than it was.

It is noted in the conclusion to the report that three officers worked on the inquiry full time for six months! What a waste of money! Had they intended to carry out a genuine, unprejudiced review they would have seen me immediately, and allowed an independent arbiter into the review team. But of course by doing this they ran the risk of uncovering too many unpalatable findings.

If an employee of the New Zealand Police transgresses internal protocols, procedures or standards, that is naturally a matter that can and should be dealt with internally, in the same way as any other organisation would deal with personnel issues. But when police activities impinge on the public, or are called into question in the public arena, I believe those issues should be dealt with totally independently. Indeed, I go so far as to say that it is the very fact that the police have been able to deal with public complaints in the way they have over the past hundred years that has caused the siege mentality that appears to exist among them.

In his book *In the Name of the Law — the Collapse of Criminal*

Justice, David Rose looks at this situation as it exists in the UK. Rose was a specialist reporter with the *Observer* in London for seven years, and his book is an extremely well-researched and thorough work. In the process of writing the book he spent a considerable amount of time with officers from the Kilburn division of London's Metropolitan Police. The main focus of the book is the role the police play in the criminal justice system in the UK. The chapter entitled 'Policing the Police' looks at the question of police accountability. The UK has had a Police Complaints Authority similar to that of New Zealand for nearly three decades, so their experience is worth our consideration.

After the Brixton riots in London in 1981 Lord Scarman, a retired English law lord, was commissioned to review the implications of those events. At the core of his report, writes Rose, were two crucial principles: that police should consult the communities they police, and that they should be accountable to those communities for their actions.

'Accountability,' Lord Scarman says, 'renders the police answerable for what they do. Thereby it prevents them from slipping into an enclosed fortress of inward thinking and social isolation which would, in the long term, result in a siege mentality — the police in their fortress (happy as long as it is secure) and the rest of us outside unhappy, uncertain and insecure (for we do not know what they will do, or how they will do it).'

The Police Complaints Board was constituted in the UK in 1976, and replaced in 1984 by a Police Complaints Authority. In his report Lord Scarman gives a damning assessment of the board's capacity to do the job of handling public complaints against the police:

People do not believe the complaint will be investigated or judged fairly, and they are worried that if they do complain they will subsequently be subjected to harassment and intimidation by the police. The chief criticisms centre on the fact that under the present system the police investigate themselves.

He concluded that confidence would never be restored 'as long as the investigation of complaints remains in police hands'. The only argument for the current system was cost, he said, which Scarman dismissed.

According to Rose, the new PCA, established in 1984, was little more than a revamp of the old board, in effect rubber-stamping police investigations into themselves. Rose writes:

In more than half of all complaints the PCA takes no role at all. In another 40% or so, the police will refer a case for possible supervision. The PCA is left with less than 1000 of the most serious cases each year (less than 10%) where one of its lay members will 'supervise' the police inquiry. They do not direct inquiries in any meaningful way. With just eight members allocated to the authority's investigations, each with more than 100 inquiries to do each year, it would be a physical impossibility [to be more involved] anyway.

It would appear that New Zealand has adopted, almost in its entirety, a system used, and failing, in Britain. For Rose goes on to explain that in its entire history the PCA in the UK has done nothing to provide accountability, restore confidence, or indeed see that a just result occurs. He found that in Britain 86 per cent of people were dissatisfied with the result of their complaint.

Here in New Zealand I have considered the cases of numerous complainants. These are people who have come to me, unsolicited, as a result of reading *David and Goliath* or seeing me on television in my fight for justice for David Bain. I have yet to meet anybody who has made a complaint against the police and been satisfied with the result. And that includes many lawyers who have complained formally on behalf of their clients. In fact, one barrister I know refers to the PCA as the 'police whitewash machine'.

The situation seems relatively simple to me. By the very nature of the work they are required to do, there are bound to be complaints against the police. Many of these, for obvious reasons, are likely to be spurious. Some may require simply an apology, an acknowledgement that procedures were not strictly adhered to, or an improvement in procedures. Some, however, may concern police malpractice, such as physical abuse, heavy-handed tactics, perjury, fabrication of evidence, or other serious charges. And some of these will be factually correct.

Many complaints in New Zealand are not vigorously pursued by the complainant, simply because they run out of the resources and willpower to fight the huge bureaucratic machine that is the police. They simply give up. In addition, most sustainable complaints against the police are settled out of court, with no admission of liability, and a confidentiality clause so nobody ever hears of them.

In order for the police to feel that public faith in them can be restored, totally independent scrutiny must be maintained. And for justice to be done, when wrongdoing is uncovered the same standards of criminal prosecution should apply to the police as to any other member of the community.

The adversarial system

I have examined the first two phases of what I call the 'process' of justice — first, the police at the coal face, responsible for investigating crimes, laying charges and making arrests, and second, the depositions hearing, the pre-trial procedure at which the case against the accused is (or is supposed to be) put forward, followed by the preparation of evidence for the trial. The final stage is the trial itself — where the advocates for each side face off in a battle to win.

This is a difficult aspect of the system for me to write about with authority, for the simple reason that I am not trained in law, and have little experience of the courtroom, the scene of the drama, thrust and counter-thrust that is the trial process.

Having said that, I have had many serious and in-depth discussions on the subject with a vast array of people who are certainly experts on the subject, which have enabled me to form some considered opinions. Two of the most highly qualified and knowledgeable of these people are Colin Withnall QC and Peter Williams QC, and I include statements of their views as appendices I and II.

In addition to the close association I have enjoyed with these two gentlemen, dating back now some four years, others with whom I have discussed the issue of the adversarial system include many criminal barristers, some District Court judges, and one of New Zealand's most prominent Crown solicitors. I have also read quite extensively on this subject, and my opinions are based on this wide cross-section of opinion and knowledge gleaned over the past four years.

In short, my view is that the adversarial trial is defective in a fundamental way because it is not designed to get to the essential truth. Corroboration of this point of view is contained in a New Zealand Law Commission research paper entitled *Juries in Criminal Trials*, written in 1999. In a section titled 'Withholding Information', it states:

> At least in part the perception of many jurors that they were not getting the full story arose because they perceived the trial in inquisitorial rather than adversarial terms. That is, they saw the trial process and their role in it as being to uncover the whole truth, including the surrounding circumstances, rather than to assess the version of events presented by the parties.

I believe this assessment unwittingly provides the clue to what may be the major failing of the adversarial system — the use of tactics by both sides to put a slant on the evidence for the purpose of disguising the real truth, or use of the laws of admissibility and relevance to disguise the picture altogether.

In his book *The Cartel — Lawyers and Their Nine Magic Tricks*, Whitton makes frequent reference to this subject and quotes extensively from prominent legalists to make his points. For example, the Honourable Gordon Samuels, governor of New South Wales and formerly a justice of the New South Wales Court of Appeal, commented in November 1996:

> Sometimes a suggestion that our system of Justice is not designed to get at the truth strikes both lay and professional persons as profoundly shocking, almost to the degree of blasphemy. But there are statements of authority in the High Court that seem to me to adopt that view.

And the Honourable Mr Justice Ian Callenan, appointed to the High Court of Australia in 1997, is quoted as saying in 1987:

> In adversary litigation the object of the parties is simple, to win the case. If in the course of winning the case the whole truth is unmistakenly ascertained and all relevant facts exposed, then a desirable but nonetheless no more than incidental result will have been achieved.

Whitton's essential theme is that since the beginning of the British (adversarial) system of justice in the thirteenth century, the 'Cartel', clever and influential lawyers, have subverted the system by bringing about the introduction of various 'rules' into the legal system that are specifically designed to hide the truth. The first of their nine magic tricks, he says, dates back to the inception of the adversarial system and is fundamental to it, creating the fallacy on which all else rests and causing the chaos that now exists. Magic trick number one, Whitton says, is 'the ludicrous notion that truth is not relevant to justice'. It seems hard to disagree!

The second magic trick, he says, is the 'jury system' — the inscrutable jury, who do not have to provide reasons for their decisions. This has always seemed perverse to me, as without reasons how can you judge the validity of a verdict? But more importantly, it was the jury system that provided the opportunity for legal rules to be created that were designed to obscure the truth from the jury (see the quote above from the Law Commission's report on juries' perceptions of trials).

Over the centuries the role of the judge has diminished to the point where the judge has essentially become an administrator of the system of legal rules governing the trial process. These rules preclude the judge from taking part in the decision-making process altogether. In the eighteenth century, says Whitton, '. . . defence lawyers persuaded dubious judges to accept an unjust and unfair form of adversary system and rules which conceal evidence and get the guilty off. Even more remarkably, lawyers persuaded judges to surrender control of trials to people whose obligation is to win — lawyers.'

Whitton goes on to say that any legal system that purports to be fair has an adversarial component. But in inquisitorial versions (that is, European) the defence lawyer (and of course the prosecution) can protect their clients' interests in every way up to the point where they might interfere with the truth. In the inquisitorial system the fact-gathering judge, who sits *with* the jury, performs the cross-examination of the witnesses and the accused. This, Whitton says, is a great engine for discovering the truth. In the hands of lawyers, it is a great engine for obscuring it.

David Rose, in his book *In the Name of the Law*, quotes the pre-eminent English criminal barrister Ron Thwaites QC:

Defendants don't ask for your judgement on them but your advocacy. There is no such thing as a hopeless case, only a hopeless barrister. If there are more acquittals than there used to be, that reflects the commitment and skill of counsel!

That may be fine in principle, but let's consider the possible ramifications by looking at what Thwaites says next:

I will acknowledge that the witness box is a very lonely place. It is very hard to withstand good cross-examination, even if you're telling the absolute truth. The art of good cross-examination is to seal all exits leaving only the chimney. Then smoke 'em out. Sometimes police officers do make innocent mistakes. It can be easy to convert mistakes into sinister lies. It's not being hard, it's not being soft. It's doing my job. You must go to the heart of the case by going for the witness — not its big toe.

So let's look at what Whitton calls the lawyers' 'nine magic tricks'.

1. *Truth not important.* It seems to me that what is important in our system is to see whether enough evidence exists to lay charges and get a conviction.

2. *The inscrutable jury.* Because juries do not provide reasons for their verdicts it is impossible to know what was in the jurors' minds. This has the effect of aborting the appeal process.

3. *The adversarial system.* The abdication of control of the trial process from the judge to the lawyers, because of the other 'magic tricks' to follow.

4. *The right of silence.* This has serious potential to advantage the guilty, and can work against the innocent if they call on it. In inquisitorial systems, the court has the absolute right to question the accused and all witnesses to try to establish the actual truth.

5. *Rule against similar facts.* It is not permissible to make the character of the accused an issue. That is, a pattern of previous convictions or behaviour can only be presented to a judge to consider in sentencing, not to a court to assist it in reaching a verdict.

6. *Rule against hearsay.* There are obvious reasons for this rule, but it invariably seems to be a source of contention, and can often lead to extremely salient evidence being discarded.

7. *The standard of proof.* The definitions of 'beyond reasonable doubt' vary from judge to judge and time to time. For further

discussion of this point, see Colin Withnall's comments in Appendix I.

8. *The Christie discretion*. This rule allows the judge to suppress evidence on the grounds that 'it is only *slightly* probative but *highly* prejudicial'. This of course relies entirely on the judge's discretion in his interpretation in the circumstances of 'slightly' and 'highly'.

9. *The exclusionary rule*. This relates to whether evidence is allowable if it has been gained improperly. It can mean that a guilty person may get off because of an indiscretion on the part of the investigators during the gathering of evidence.

While Whitton's concept is largely a comment on the system in Australia, it draws on a vast historical perspective whence that system originated. One last comment of Whitton's, which I believe to be very true, is that law students are not taught the origins of the system they are trained in, resulting in vast ignorance. Law schools teach their students how to use the legal system, which they naturally accept as a valid system. It seems that it is only after years of experience that disillusion sets in and a lawyer even begins to consider the concept, 'What validity does a justice system have if it is based on the fundamental principle that the truth is only incidental to the process?'

This point will no doubt incense judges, legalists and politicians in this country, as it has in Great Britain and Australia. But, like it or not, it is the fact of the matter. As Colin Withnall QC concludes in his paper, 'Only when that question [the topic I have been addressing] has been answered, should the detail [of change] be addressed.'

David Rose is clearly in no doubt about the problems created by the adversarial system as we know it in the UK and New

Zealand. He is scathing in his assessment of the criminal justice system in the UK, on many fronts. He comments that the hierarchical class structure that has developed, with criminals the only group below the police, and High Court and Appeal Court judges reclusively and without accountability dispensing justice from on high, is a natural, albeit unsatisfactory, side effect of the historical growth of the British system. He comments that politicians, and often the most influential ones, are made up disproportionately of lawyers. This certainly applies in New Zealand, and means that change to the system is inordinately difficult to bring about.

He comments that class wealth and status have, or at least are seen to have, an impact on proceedings that is unfair and unjust. The more money an accused has, the better the legal team and the more cunning the argument. The courts seem to take a much dimmer view of the lower-class, 'casual' criminal than of the white collar professional criminal.

While these inequalities are endemic, Rose states, they do not signal a crisis or collapse in the system. They simply represent the way the game has been played for centuries. However, he is much less generous in his assessment of the workings and results achieved by the system in the modern era (and remember, *In the Name of the Law* was published in the UK in 1996), stating:

> But the contemporary crisis in criminal justice is not simply a matter of increasing demands. The system is failing in its first and most essential task: to separate the 'factually guilty' criminals from the falsely accused.

Many of Rose's observations will no doubt be viewed as verging on heresy in this country. He says, for example:

219

As they [critics of the adversarial trial] rightly point out, adversarial justice is not a search for the truth. It does not pretend to be an objective inquiry. Each side, prosecution and defence, has its role to play: to *construct* [my italic] its case and win.

Like me, Rose believes that not only is the trial process itself flawed, but that the pre-trial investigation stage of the process comes under extreme pressure as a result of the adversarial process. He goes on to write:

The police, just as much as the wily or ruthless counsel for the defence, operate with the rules of adversarial justice constantly in mind. The adversarial mindset exerts a further deeper influence, visible at the very centre of police culture. No less than barristers, the police want and need to win the contest, to 'get a result'. However much chief officers may exhort detectives to work impartially with open minds, every institution within adversarial criminal justice exerts pressure in the opposite direction.

And again:

If police work is to fit with the rest of the system, it can no more be a 'search for the truth', than the contested trial. It has to be about constructing cases, and gathering evidence around a probable suspect. By definition it leaves no room for objectivity.

The inquisitorial system

According to Rose, it is in the pre-trial phase of the process that the inquisitorial system has the greatest advantage over the adversarial system.

The essential element of the inquisitorial system that distinguishes it from our system is that it is designed to be and operates as a simple, objective search for the truth. Although all parties can, and do, have legal representation, the search for truth is not impeded by complex legal rules, the need to win, or the presumption of innocence in the face of a charge of guilty. The 'contest' is taken out of the proceedings.

One simple way of explaining this difference is to compare a trial with a game of rugby. In rugby there are rules, a referee, and so on — much like a trial in the adversarial system. Like a trial, the players must adhere to the rules or they are penalised. Like a trial, the referee (judge) must be scrupulous in his understanding and application of the rules. Often, in important encounters, sides will use tactics to get around the rules and confuse the opposition, in order to gain an advantage for the purpose of winning the match. The most serious matches often become grim, uninteresting encounters, where the real skills of the players are not even on show as the game becomes a close contest where neither side takes chances, both simply looking for that single mistake or transgression that will give them the edge on the scoreboard.

Contrast this to the festival match, that traditional pre-season warm-up Barbarians fixture. Here tries are scored, the referee turns a blind eye to the odd knock-on, and the teams are not preoccupied with winning. What we see is usually the opposite of the 'serious' game described above — running, swerving, impromptu athletic brilliance and ball skills abound. A form of 'purism', of untarnished, joyful expression takes over, delighted in by participants and spectators alike. Sport in its most pure form.

The analogy I see is that the test match is akin to the adversarial system, and the festival match to the inquisitorial system. In the test match, skill, spontaneity, a carefree style, sportsmanship and fair play are often the losers, because winning is all that counts. The essence of the game, of sport itself, is destroyed by the 'need to win'. The festival game has no such constraints and so a pure sporting occasion is the result. The inquisitorial system, having removed the element of 'contest', and not permitting anyone to take sides — with 'not guilty' on one side, and 'accused' on the other — is able to concentrate on discovering the truth — getting back to what should be the most essential element of any justice system.

How does the inquisitorial system achieve this?

Basically, what happens is that immediately a serious crime is committed, a person who in the French inquisitorial system is called a *'juge d'instruction'*, and who I shall call a 'judicial official', is appointed to oversee and supervise the gathering of evidence, and is closely associated with the police in this exercise. This 'judicial officer' is trained specifically in investigative techniques, and interviews witnesses and suspects. As evidence is gathered, lawyers acting for suspects are provided by him with a full dossier of the evidence against them, and they can request that further specific enquiries be made.

Any propensity on the part of a detective or the police force as an entity to form a mindset against a particular person is foiled during the investigation. Undercover activities have to be

222

approved and monitored by the judicial officer. The fiascos that occurred in the cases I have recounted in this book could not have happened under such a system.

During the trial itself, the jury, if there is one, sits with the trial judges. After the witnesses have given their evidence only the judges, with the help of the jury, can cross-examine. This has the effect of eliciting information from the witness with the aim of getting at the essential truth, rather than in our system where cross-examination is more often designed to destroy the witness.

In the early 1990s, a Royal Commission was set up in the UK to look at the justice system in the light of the number of serious miscarriages of justice that were surfacing. This study found that in neither France nor Germany, where an inquisitorial system is used, would such miscarriages as the convictions of the Guildford four or the Birmingham six be likely to occur.

In addition, the 26-page report concluded that in those jurisdictions a high level of cooperation and mutual trust existed between the parties — that is, the police, defence lawyers, prosecutors and judges. The Royal Commission also commented that public confidence in the justice system was high in both France and Germany, and that conviction rates were extremely high in both countries.

However, the Commission completely rejected the idea of adopting any aspects of the continental systems on the grounds of cultural and historical perspectives. Rose comments that this is hardly surprising, since the witnesses to the Commission were almost entirely from one part or another of the existing British system. Nobody I have read, including Withnall, Whitton and Rose, suggests a wholesale adoption of the French or German system.

However, I am very firmly of the opinion that the current

system is fundamentally flawed and totally inadequate to deal with the issues confronting modern society in relation to criminal justice. Flawed, because the system we have creates and exerts pressures on all parties to adopt a confrontational approach, leading inevitably to miscarriages of justice, and lengthy, unnecessary and costly appeals, retrials and waste of police and court time. Inadequate, because the increase in crime, and the increase in the failure to detect crime, continues unabated.

The police are almost forced into the role of protagonists, instead of simply being investigators seeking the truth. This inevitably leads to highly questionable jury trials which leave the public feeling uncertain and disillusioned.

John Barlow had to go through three trials before he was convicted, finally faced with a Crown team that was relentless against him, plugging the holes with each new trial, and a jury who could not possibly have been free of prejudice. I have grave doubts as to the safety of his convictions.

Peter Ellis served out his entire sentence before finally a restricted inquiry was ordered. It appears unlikely that justice will be done, regardless of the inquiry's findings. He is getting too little, too late.

David Dougherty is still fighting for compensation after being wrongfully convicted, and that process has been going on for three years. I will never forget Doug Graham saying at the time of Dougherty's acquittal, 'Just because he's been found not guilty, that doesn't mean he's innocent.'!

David Bain's case has now been before the Governor-General for over two years. Our battle continues, and I'm sure will ultimately be successful, because truth, that ingredient so elusive to those who are involved in the justice system in this country, will eventually prevail.

In June 2000 I believe there were twelve other petitions before the Governor-General and being investigated by the Justice Department! Surely this is indicative of the problems of which I write.

Time to act

It is high time the powers that be recognised the failings of the current set-up; recognised that what is happening in similar jurisdictions overseas is also happening here.

Put personalities, egos and precious systems aside, I say. Some real and drastic steps need to be taken. In my view these include, but are not limited to, the institution of an independent Police Complaints Authority with teeth and guts. This would immediately provide some solace to the people whose lives become tragically affected by the failings of our police, and ultimately it would benefit the police themselves. In 1998 and 1999, the police were the subjects of claims by New Zealand citizens totalling over 17.5 million dollars. These were resolved by the police paying $672,041.61 in confidential, out-of-court settlements, with no admission of liability on their part.

A second immediate improvement that would have a significant impact on crime detection and conviction would be to appoint a person, or a body, separate from both the police and the Crown prosecution agencies, to oversee investigations leading up to depositions or pre-trial hearings. This role is that referred to earlier as the judicial officer. Police investigation teams would have to be answerable to this person, and this would have a number of desirable effects. Firstly, it would ensure objectivity, preventing the mindset referred to by Judge Callander from developing. Secondly, it would take considerable pressure off the police and allow them to return to their primary roles of crime prevention and detection. Thirdly, it would provide a buffer between the police and the Crown prosecutors, and other Crown agencies such as the ESR who, like it or not, inevitably fall into the role of 'de facto' police allies. Fourthly, and very importantly, it would be the judicial officer's responsibility to ensure that 'full and timely disclosure' is made to the eventual accused's counsel.

Who or what type of person should fill this role? Perhaps the first thing to look at is who should not fill it. They should not be drawn from former police staff, nor from the judiciary, for the simple reason that both these sectors have a preconditioned view which I believe would be undesirable and inappropriate. To use accounting parlance, the role is more that of an auditor. I believe specific training should be available to professional people who would either apply for it or be invited to participate. They could then be appointed either on a full-time basis, or simply on an 'as required' basis.

I believe these two simple changes — the institution of a Police Complaints Authority with teeth and muscle, and that of a judicial officer to 'oversee' police in serious crime investigation — would go a long way to ensuring that the eventual trial would then have the full set of facts available to argue out.

The third fundamental change I would like to see is a revamp of the trial process itself in a few specific ways.

Firstly, I believe the bench should have more power over the protagonists to ensure that the truth does not become lost in the process of the trial itself. This could be achieved by having all serious criminal trials presided over by a leading judge, who is assisted by two other judges and nine jurors selected from the public forum, all of whom sit together, and who have the power to put questions to witnesses. One of the benefits of this would relate to expert witnesses. With the increasing use of scientific evidence in criminal inquiries these days, ranging from DNA analysis to sophisticated ballistics and blood splatter patterns, it must be well nigh impossible at times for juries to make any sense of it. It is even more difficult when, as is often the case, each side calls an expert on the same subject, who each proffer different views. A jury made up as I am suggesting, with the power to question witnesses, may wish to analyse the evidence given by such experts, and then recall them to clarify particular points so that they can feel satisfied that the salient evidence can be given its proper weight.

The judge in charge would then perform the dual role, as he does in the District Court and in most civil proceedings, of judge and jury. The decision could then be given in writing, with the other two judges taking responsibility for confirming the verdict with a concise and reasoned response.

If an appeal was then made on matters of fact (not appealable under the current situation except in extreme cases, because of the inscrutable jury), the issue to be appealed would be obvious.

A good example of where this might apply is the John Barlow case. It was the defence position in this case that the pistol Barlow disposed of in the tip was not the murder weapon. They called expert ballistic evidence to support this proposition. The Crown argued that this pistol was indeed the murder weapon. It seems that the matter was never resolved either way.

Now we have no way of knowing what weight the jury placed on any of this evidence. Did it even matter to them in making their decision? We shall never know. Barlow argues that if they had accepted that the pistol was not the murder weapon, he would not have been convicted, but we cannot be certain of that. If the jury had given a written verdict in which they stated that they relied on the fact that this was the murder weapon, then Barlow would be in a position to appeal their decision if he could prove, for example, that it was not. Another example could be the witness Denise Laney in the Bain case, the last person to see David before he completed his paper round. A jury with more authority may have demanded to hear from her in person, she being such an important witness.

So, to me, a jury of nine laypeople, two assistant judges and a presiding judge, or some development along these lines, who are required to provide a brief explanation of their verdict in writing, would be a huge advance.

Many people with whom I have spoken are uneasy about Scott Watson's conviction. Suspicious hairs, secret witnesses and missing ketches add to that concern. John Barlow had to undergo three trials before he was convicted, and many commentators have expressed concerns about his conviction also. I have yet to meet a barrister in New Zealand who does not believe that Peter Ellis' conviction should have been overturned. Rex Haig is another, convicted of murder on the flimsiest of evidence. We don't need any more Janine Law or Wicked Willies cases. Are these prominent examples just the tip of the iceberg?

On the other hand, professional criminals are having a field-day in their life of crime. If they get caught at all they have a real chance of escaping conviction.

The time for change is now. It is no use tinkering with what we've got, which is a system that has largely been unchanged for centuries. I say, let's be bold, let's be non-partisan, let's design a procedure that is founded on the principle that without truth there can be no justice.

The finish — for now

In April 1998, about five months after the publication of the police/PCA report, I was served with papers giving notice of civil proceedings against me as first defendant, and Reed Publishing (NZ) Ltd as second defendant.

The claimants were Detective Sergeant Milton Weir of Dunedin, Detective Sergeant Kevin Anderson of Balclutha (formerly of Dunedin), and another police officer whose claim was trifling (as his name was not even mentioned in the book, and whose claim was settled out of court). Weir's claim was for compensatory damages of $200,000, punitive damages of $50,000, costs and any other relief deemed just in the circumstances. Anderson claimed $150,000 compensation, $30,000 punitive damages, plus costs and other relief. The third claimant claimed $95,000, bringing the total amount to $525,000, plus costs. It soon became apparent that the Police Association (the police union, headed up by Greg O'Connor) was meeting the claimants' costs.

Weir claimed that he had been defamed in the book *David and Goliath* because, he stated, the ordinary reader of the book would take from it that:

a. he had planted the glasses lens;
b. he had committed perjury in the High Court trial of David Bain;

c. he was part of a conspiracy with other officers to secure David's conviction by giving false evidence; and

d. he is a dishonest person, corrupt and unfit to be a member of the police.

Anderson's claims were essentially the same as points (b), (c) and (d) above.

The first thing required of me was to issue a statement of defence, which had to be done almost immediately. This turned out to be a massive undertaking in itself, as the laws of defamation are extremely complex. Few New Zealand lawyers are experienced in this type of proceedings.

I was referred to Julian Miles QC, who is considered one of New Zealand's foremost specialists in this field. And so began what was for a long time a slightly prickly relationship, for the reason that Mr Miles, like many others in his profession, took a rather sceptical view of my book and therefore me personally, which was that my stance on David Bain was superficial, ill-informed and opportunistic. Despite this, however, we worked away together, with me struggling to understand the defamation laws. The biggest obstacle was separating the knowledge that was available about the Bain case at this time from what I knew and what was in my mind at the time I wrote the book.

Anyway, eventually we got there, at very considerable cost, which Reed Publishing and I agreed to share. It was at this point that we got lucky, since Reed had an insurance policy for exactly this eventuality which covered not only themselves, but also the author! It had already been pointed out to me that the cost of defending these claims would probably be in excess of $200,000, and of course if we lost we would have to meet the claimants' costs as well!

While the insurance policy was a great relief, it was something of a double-edged sword, as it seemed likely that the insurers would want to settle the claims out of court. They did actually make an offer to the claimants, who agreed to accept if I would publicly apologise to them as well. This I rejected entirely — I recall saying at the time, 'They can throw me inside before I'll do that.'

At about this time I became aware that the police had hired private investigators to monitor my affairs and, it would seem, generally check me out. I would have thought my life and views were pretty much public knowledge by then — perhaps this tactic, along with the defamation case itself, was designed to wear me down and frighten me off.

Various people around the country were contacted by these investigators, including my former wife. All in all, it was a pretty daunting situation. If anything, though, it only served to deepen my resolve. The attitude I adopted was essentially that people don't usually behave this way unless they are a bit desperate.

The actual trial finally began in late May 2000, and ran for two weeks. During the pre-trial hearing there were several significant rulings. We lost a major point, but in general it quickly became evident even at this stage that the claimants were going to be in pretty deep trouble.

The point we lost can be put down to Justice Noel Anderson, the presiding judge, exercising his discretion in an extremely fair way — overriding a technical hitch created by the plaintiffs in their most significant claim. They had claimed that the book said the glasses lens was planted 'in the position in which Weir gave evidence that he had found it'. This claim had no hope of succeeding because the book actually stated that the lens was never at any time in the position that he said in evidence that he had found it in! So how could it also say that the lens was planted there?

Julian Miles moved to have this claim struck out altogether, because it could not possibly stand up. Severely embarrassed, Don Mathieson QC, counsel for the claimants, said the claim should have stated 'planted somewhere in Stephen's bedroom'. Justice Anderson allowed the amendment, and at the same time advised that in his opinion the book was capable of carrying the meaning of the amended version of the claim.

My alarm and consternation were twofold. First, I had been advised that such an important amendment would be unlikely to be granted at such a late stage, and thus we had not bothered to construct any defence to either version. Second, it indicated to me that perhaps I was going to draw the short straw whenever the judge's discretion was called into play during the proceedings. As it turned out, that was not the case, and my eventual assessment of the judge was that proceedings were administered very fairly and properly.

On almost every other front, though, we seemed to be ahead. Vast sections of the plaintiffs' evidence and, in three cases, the witnesses' entire evidence, were struck out altogether.

One thing that amazed me was that the plaintiffs did not call even one person to say he or she had read the book and found that the reputations of the claimants had been demeaned. In fact, for the most part the witnesses they called began by saying that they had *not* read the book!

In relation to Weir and Anderson's evidence Julian and I, with Colin Withnall's assistance, had spent many days preparing for their cross-examination. I couldn't wait for Julian to get them on the stand. The former Detective Sergeant Weir gave his evidence, which was all fine and dandy until the cross-examination began, when it was exposed for the nonsense it was by the clinical questioning of Julian Miles. Concessions came thick and fast. At times he laid the blame on other officers involved in the murder inquiry. His main evidence takes up 32 pages of the trial transcript, and his cross-examination 52 pages, which equated to about a full day on the stand.

Weir made some major admissions:

— He admitted that the key photograph, photo 62 in the Bain trial, was not shown at the depositions hearing, and not discussed with David Bain's counsel, Michael Guest.

— He admitted that what he had claimed under oath at the Bain trial to be the 'lens' in photo 62 was not a lens.

— He admitted that the photo did not show where he found the lens.

— He admitted that his evidence was wrong.

— He agreed that he was 'shocked' when he found out that the timing evidence to do with the computer given at the Bain trial was wrong.

He dug himself a really nice hole when he stated in his evidence that he was called on to the inquiry team for Operation TAM (the investigation into the disappearance of Olivia Hope and Ben Smart), but was, he said, barred from being involved in any type of scene investigation. He said this was because of the 'unfair' slight on his character resulting from the allegations in *David and Goliath*. This aspect of his evidence was covered on *3 News* that evening. Just as I was dozing off to sleep that night, my cellphone rang. It was Mr Watson, Scott's father, whom I had never previously spoken to. He said, 'Your Mr Weir, I saw him on the news. That's a whole lot of bull. He was in charge of a group of detectives who searched our house on four occasions in January 1998.' He then gave me the dates. The following day

Julian Miles asked Weir whether searching a house fell into the category of doing scene investigations. Weir agreed that it did. Miles then put to Weir that he had conducted scene searches of the Watson house. Reluctantly Weir conceded that he had been involved in those scene searches.

Detective Sergeant Anderson, for his part, made what I considered to be a more forthright attempt to explain his actions during the Bain case. He made several references to Senior Sergeant Jim Doyle as being the officer responsible for preparing the evidence for the Bain trial.

Anderson was also cross-examined for nearly a day, and made many significant admissions. In relation to his own evidence at the Bain trial he conceded that he knew that his watch had been checked for accuracy, and that he knew the result of that check. However, he maintained that even though he knew of this inaccuracy, and that it related to a critical issue, it was not his duty to include it in his evidence. The following exchange then took place:

JULIAN MILES: Even though you knew it was inaccurate?
DS ANDERSON: If I had been asked whether my watch was . . . fast I would have answered it.
JULIAN MILES: Are you saying it was up to the defence to correct your evidence?
DS ANDERSON: No, what I'm saying is that at that time I gave my evidence the fact that my watch was out wasn't part of it.
JULIAN MILES: You prepared it, didn't you?
DS ANDERSON: Yes I did.

In other words, he said that he only needed to tell the whole truth if he was asked to.

Anyway, the evidence of the plaintiffs was completed with their case appearing to be in disarray. In all they called seven witnesses, apart from themselves, including their wives, three other officers from the Bain inquiry, Rob Pope (who became well known as the head of Operation TAM, the investigation into the disappearance of Olivia Hope and Ben Smart), and former Assistant Commissioner Brion Duncan, who was in charge of the police/PCA review into the 'allegations' in *David and Goliath*.

My evidence was lengthy, and I was cross-examined for over a day. I enjoyed it. I had been looking forward to the day when the truth of the contents of *David and Goliath* could be publicly put to the test. It appeared to me, as the day wore on, that Mr Mathieson, counsel for the plaintiffs, was having more trouble with me than I was with him.

By this stage the punitive damages claims had been dropped, since they were clearly untenable, and three of the other claims had also fallen by the wayside, leaving only five claims. The jury dismissed four of those, including all of Anderson's claims and Weir's 'planting' claim, on the grounds that the book did not carry the meanings alleged. With regard to the allegation that the book carried the meaning that Weir committed perjury during David Bain's High Court trial, the jury said that it did. In my evidence I had stated that I believed Mr Weir 'in all probability knew that it was wrong'.

This matter was put to the jury by the judge in the following way:

Do the words complained of in their natural and ordinary meaning when read together and in the context of *David and Goliath* as a whole, mean that Mr Weir committed perjury at the High Court trial of David Bain for the murders?

The jury answered yes to this question, which required them

to respond to the next question, which was:

Is such meaning an expression of 'opinion' in the legal sense?

To which they also answered yes, which led to the question:

Is such an expression of opinion based on facts alleged in the book?

To which they also answered yes, which led to the final question on this issue:

Are such facts proved to be true or not materially different from the truth?

To which they also answered yes.

The jury's affirmative response to these questions meant that I was entitled to my honest opinion that Weir had committed perjury because it was underpinned by supporting facts in the book which *had been proven to be true during the trial*.

This trial achieved in two weeks what four years of work had failed to do. It demonstrated once and for all that my analysis of many of the central issues of the Bain proceedings was neither superficial, nor biased, nor materially inaccurate. The sworn testimony under cross-examination of the very officers themselves endorsed this reality.

The police/PCA report's vindication of all of the officers involved in the Bain inquiry undoubtedly fuelled the confidence of the plaintiffs and the Police Association in bringing this action against me. The trial demonstrated once and for all that the report, though, was in some crucial respects fallacious. The very accusations levelled at me by the plaintiffs, of being biased, superficial and inaccurate, can now, I believe, fairly and squarely be laid on the report itself.

A complete analysis of the testimony given during this trial is being provided to the Minister of Justice, Phil Goff, to support our claims that David Bain is innocent and should be pardoned.

The judgement was agreed to by Don Mathieson QC for the plaintiffs, and costs awarded against them. I imagine the total cost to the Police Association will comfortably exceed $500,000.

If there is some supernatural power guiding life on this earth, then it surely showed its hand when the police sought to muzzle me by issuing these proceedings.

Julian Miles QC was magnificent. We worked together passionately, and in the end I believe we developed great mutual respect. There is nothing more uplifting than seeing a true professional at work, and I am indebted to the police for giving me that opportunity during the trial. The rates charged by such people appear on the face of it to be exorbitant. But when they are compared, for example, to what comparable expertise on the sportsfield earns, I would disagree. Julian was emotionally and mentally drained when he uttered the final words of his impassioned and brilliantly constructed final address. He had given his all.

Paul Grimshaw, his junior, played an insignificant role in the trial, but early on it was his belief in me and my book that persuaded the insurers not to settle out of court, and I thank him for that.

I also thank Reed Publishing (NZ) Ltd for having the guts to publish the book and for supporting me throughout as they have.

Finally, I take my hat off to my great friend, ally and mentor in Dunedin, Colin Withnall QC. He has been with me all the way, and spent countless hours helping me to prepare for this trial. He truly is a credit to his profession and, even more significantly as far as I am concerned, a man of great principle and enormous integrity.

Between us, I am sure Colin and I will achieve the ultimate

goal that we had in mind four years ago when we set out on this mission. We will ensure that truth shall be the winner. The truth being that the entire process involving the investigation, prosecution and defence of David Bain simply went off the rails, with the subsequent inevitable result that David, too, became enveloped in the 'false fabric of guilt'.

David Bain Appeal Fund

David Bain's petition seeking a pardon from the Governor-General was lodged on 16 June 1998. At the time of publication of this book, J. Karam and C.S. Withnall QC are still working with the Ministry of Justice on a broad range of issues, relating to the petition.

This is costly and time consuming.

Donations can be made to:

'David Bain Appeal Fund'
c/- O'Driscoll & Marks
Barristers and Solicitors
PO Box 639
Dunedin

Copies of *David and Goliath* can be obtained from the same address for $22.00 including post and packaging.

All donations will be gratefully accepted by David Bain and his supporters.

Appendix I

Reform of the criminal justice system — a view from the coal face

Colin Withnall QC

(First published in the *Otago Law Review* special issue to mark the 125th Anniversary of Otago Law School; Volume 9, No. 2, 1998.) Colin Withnall QC is a Dunedin barrister. He was a part-time lecturer in the Otago Law Faculty from 1978 to 1987.

I Introduction

In the past decade the process of investigation and prosecution of serious crime has come under increasing critical public scrutiny. In a number of high profile cases there has been much public criticism of the competence, integrity and fairness of police investigations and of the trial process itself. Concerns expressed range across the whole spectrum from simple negligence or incompetence to deliberate presentation of false evidence, whether directly by the commission of perjury or indirectly by the suppression of or failure to disclose evidence which contradicts that given by witnesses.

II Historical Perspective

Such allegations are not a modern phenomenon. Generations of defence lawyers, in the days when disclosure of information on the police file was the exception rather than the rule, frequently heard such allegations from their clients and from witnesses but the avenues of exploration were virtually closed other than through counsel's forensic skills in cross-examination.

Complaints of police malpractice could only be made to the police and were investigated by the police themselves. The results were entirely predictable. Invariably, the result was that the complaint was found to have no substance, the police hierarchy preferring the version of events related by the police officers concerned to that of the complainant and any supporting witnesses. The author recalls vividly one particular incident when a complaint was made on behalf of clients and was referred to an officer new to the district to investigate. The official result of the investigation as communicated by the then District Commander was that there was no substance in any of the allegations and the police were entirely blameless. The officer who had conducted the investigation confided confidentially to the author that his recommendation had been that at least two officers should be charged with criminal offences.

Tales of threats and other inducements to obtain confessions were commonplace but were firmly denied by the officers concerned. The practice of 'firming on the verbals' was well known to defence counsel; commonly, a police officer would go into the witness box and solemnly relate certain verbal admissions claimed to have been made by the accused. Unless the officer had, in the course of giving evidence, referred to notes made at the time to refresh memory there was no means of access to any written records to check the veracity of such claims. The only course open to defence counsel then was the futile exercise of putting it to the officer in cross-examination that he was not telling the truth, and then calling one's client who would deny ever having made such statements. The result of that process was that there was a stark conflict between the evidence of the police officer and that of the defendant. In the summary jurisdiction, the way in which this conflict was resolved was by the presiding magistrate, or latterly District Court Judge, intoning the words:

I have seen and heard the witnesses. I accept the evidence of the police officer and reject the evidence of the defendant.

In the indictable jurisdiction, the defendant may have had a marginally greater chance of being believed by the jury but the prosecutors did, and still do, seize upon any conflict between the evidence of an accused person or a defence witness and a police officer with glee, exhorting the jury to consider that the police officer had absolutely no motivation other than to tell the truth in the matter and, in any event, was absolutely sober at the time in question, whereas often the defendant or the defence witness had been drinking shortly before the events in question.

III Recent Developments

1 Video and Audio Recordings

The use of video and audio recordings of interviews has been a significant advance in ensuring that oppressive means are not used in obtaining admissions. The use of these recordings is also beneficial to law enforcement agencies as a protection against unwarranted and unfounded allegations of the use of oppressive means to obtain confessions and admissions. The use of such recordings is, however, not mandatory although it is notable that the Serious Fraud Office routinely, and perhaps invariably, makes audio recordings of all interviews.

2 The Duty of Disclosure

The development of the modern obligation of disclosure in criminal cases, which effectively began with the decision in *R* v *Mason*[1] and developed through the enactment of the Official

Information Act 1982, cases such as *Commissioner of Police* v *Ombudsman*,[2] and the subsequent enactment of the Privacy Act 1993, has done much to enable such allegations to be investigated on behalf of defendants. The declaration of the rights to a fair trial and adequate time and facilities to prepare a defence embodied in section 25 of the New Zealand Bill of Rights Act 1990 has also had an important influence on this development.

It is now generally accepted by the courts that, quite apart from the express statutory provisions, there is a general duty of disclosure resting on the prosecution in the interests of securing a fair trial. The duty to disclose is not necessarily dependent upon there having been a request for disclosure by the defence, although there is no consistent line of authority in this respect.

The benefits of proper disclosure to the defence are by no means limited to ascertaining the veracity and/or admissibility of alleged confessions or admissions. Access to records of initial interviews enables defence counsel to check if witnesses have changed their evidence and to cross-examine on prior inconsistent statements to an extent not previously possible. Evidence of observations of physical evidence such as locations of objects, movements, times and sequence of discovery, including photographic and videotape evidence, are now subject to the disclosure obligation, and can provide valuable sources of evidential material to defence counsel. Such material not only provides a valuable check on the veracity of the prosecution evidence, but may also provide alternative explanations for events. Access to all this information promotes the goals of ascertaining the truth, of ensuring a fair trial and thereby enhancing public confidence in the integrity of the system.

For many years prior to the development of the modern duty of disclosure, an agreement had been and still is in place between the Commissioner of Police and the New Zealand Law Society regarding defence access to examinations by the Institute of Environmental Science and Research (ESR) and its predecessor the Department of Scientific and Industrial Research (DSIR). The full text of this agreement is published as an appendix to the Society's *Rules of Professional Conduct for Barristers and Solicitors*. Its main points, however, are that all requests for information concerning work carried out for the police by the ESR are to be made through the prosecutor; prosecutors are to advise the defence *on request* of the *general findings* of an analysis, and if a written report has been provided by the ESR, a copy will be supplied. If the defence requires to ascertain what general technique was used, a written request is to be made and a written reply will be supplied through the prosecutor. If a test favours the defence a copy is to be made available immediately without the necessity for a request. There is provision for tests to be carried out by the ESR upon request by the defence unless after consultation with the prosecutor good reason exists for refusal, although the defence will not be permitted as of right to test actual exhibits.

The limitations on full disclosure in this agreement are unsatisfactory for a number of reasons. Often it will be of importance to know what was *not* tested, and to know the results of observations made or tests carried out which are not the subject of any evidence or of any written report. Specifics of testing — e.g. composition, age, strength of control samples or sera or standard solutions, and disclosure of the precise steps and analytical techniques used — may be required to allow defence analysts to provide another opinion. This information is or should be recorded in the ESR laboratory and case notes. Accreditation of a laboratory by International Accreditation New Zealand (formerly TELARC), the body charged with setting and monitoring standards of scientific laboratories, requires that recording be of sufficient standard to allow another researcher to follow and if necessary replicate the entire test sequence. Failure to comply renders the analysis itself of doubtful value. These shortcomings in the agreement should, at least in theory, have been overtaken by the ambit of the duty of disclosure now articulated by the courts.

In civil proceedings, there is a heavy onus resting on the legal advisers to the parties to ensure proper compliance with the obligation of discovery. In criminal cases the obligation to disclose is that of the prosecuting agency and not that of the prosecutor. The prosecution guidelines issued by the Crown Law Office in Wellington as at March 1992 state:

10.11.1 Crown Solicitors are not part of a department or organisation and are not therefore subject to the Official Information Act 1982. While, as a matter of practical convenience, they may facilitate responses to requests for information they are not, as a matter of law, obliged to do so. The responsibility to provide information rests on the Police or other prosecuting agency and requests made of a Crown Solicitor should be referred to them. The Crown Solicitor should be advised of all information supplied to other parties.

10.11.2 Personal information, i.e., that particular category of official information held about an identifiable person, is the subject of an explicit right of access upon request given to that person unless it comes within some limited exceptions. Relevance is not the test under the Official Information Act.

The excerpts just quoted are taken from Appendix B to the Law Commission's Preliminary Paper No. 28 *Criminal Prosecution* published in March 1997. Since the coming into force of the Privacy Act 1993 the disclosure of personal information is controlled by the Act. Privacy Principle 6 provides for the right of an individual to have access to personal information held by 'an agency'. The definition of 'agency' includes any person or body of persons, corporate or unincorporated and whether in the public sector or the private sector subject to certain specified exceptions. Those exceptions do not include Crown Solicitors.

Presumably, the prosecution guidelines as published in the Law Commission's Report were current at the date of publication. If so, it appears that there is a distinct likelihood that the obligations of Crown Solicitors under the Privacy Act may not have been brought to their attention and the guidelines are misleading and in need of amendment.

Unfortunately, experience has shown and continues to show that the existence of the duty of disclosure does not necessarily and always result in full compliance with it. Regrettably, there continue to be cases where non-disclosure is deliberate. Recently disclosure was made for the first time of a series of photographs concerning an important issue in a case. The police had previously stated that these photographs had not 'come out'. Significantly, these photographs contradicted evidence given at the trial in relation to the picture they had been intended to record. In a recent case involving an allegation of manslaughter made against the proprietor of a Night Club in Christchurch a statement made by a witness that a person other than the accused was responsible was destroyed by the police, and the fact that it had existed was never disclosed. The reason given was that the policeman did not believe the statement. The defence subsequently learnt that the statement had been taken and the witness was subsequently interviewed, confirmed his statement and, following further investigation by an ex-police officer now working as a private investigator, the accused was discharged under section 347 of the Crimes Act 1961 — which is deemed to be an acquittal.

Unlike discovery in civil cases there is no obligation to certify on oath that the existence of all relevant documents has been disclosed to the other party (including documents in respect of which privilege against disclosing the contents may be claimed and the grounds upon which privilege is claimed).

In a criminal case, the difficulty facing defence counsel in endeavouring to ensure that proper disclosure is made is the absence of any process whereby any check can be made on the adequacy of disclosure. Put another way, one does not know what it is that one does not know. Sometimes omissions are obvious: e.g. a document may refer to another document which has not been disclosed. Sometimes witnesses will be able to say that photographs were taken or persons interviewed of which there is no record on the documents disclosed. Likewise, an understanding of some of the procedures of criminal and forensic investigation will equip defence counsel with the knowledge that experts will usually have working notes recording their observations, experiments etc. from which their reports and ultimately their evidence has been derived. These original source documents are a useful and, indeed, necessary basis against which to check the reports and evidence subsequently proffered — in the same way as the policeman's handwritten notebook entries need to be checked against subsequent job sheets, briefs of evidence etc. Original laboratory notes are essential for a scientist to check the procedures and resulting conclusions of the Crown's scientific experts. Frequently, however, these source documents, other than the policeman's notebook, are simply never provided following a general request for discovery and it seems that many counsel are unaware that these documents exist and are often fundamental to the chain of evidence which flows from them.

Apart from these situations where counsel have actual knowledge of the existence of other material or may reasonably assume that it exists, there is simply no way of knowing what other material may be in the possession of the police and has not been disclosed either deliberately or inadvertently. In many instances, non-disclosure may occur because the police officer or officers concerned do not consider the documents relevant, or where the documents are in the hands of, for instance, an expert witness engaged by the police, because it does not occur to them that they are in the possession of the police in the wider sense and ought to be disclosed.

The only sanction currently available to ensure proper compliance with the duty of disclosure is that subsequent discovery of non-disclosure may lead an Appellate Court, either on the hearing of an appeal or on a reference to it by the Governor-General under section 406 of the Crimes Act, to decide that non-disclosure has resulted in the lack of a fair trial and/or a miscarriage of justice and set aside the conviction and/or order a new trial. As a remedy for the defendant this reactive process may be less than satisfactory in a number of respects. In particular, it will only arise after a conviction if the timely disclosure would or would have been likely to result in an acquittal or the discontinuance of the proceedings before trial. The law, as it presently stands, offers little prospect of proper compensation for the consequences of a wrongful conviction.[3]

There is an urgent need for the disclosure process to be made subject to independent scrutiny and verification, and for effective and meaningful sanctions for non-compliance.

3 *The Proposal to Abolish Depositions*

The function of the preliminary hearing or depositions is to determine whether there is a *prima facie* case against a defendant. Whilst the courts have recognised that the preliminary hearing may serve a useful purpose to the defence in enabling it to explore the strengths and weaknesses of the prosecution's case, no legally enforceable right exists in the defendant to insist that all the evidence to be called at trial is called at the depositions. The prosecutor has complete discretion as to which witnesses will be called at depositions and, hence, can select the minimum number required to establish the constituent elements of a *prima facie* case.

It has, at least in some parts of the country, become increasingly common for prosecutors to adopt this tactic. In an extreme case, *R* v *Haig*,[4] the Crown had provided deposition statements in respect of 62 witnesses. The defence agreed to the admission by consent of 24 of these statements on the basis that the remaining witnesses would be called at depositions. Those 24 statements were duly admitted. The Crown called 11 of the remaining 38 witnesses to give evidence and then announced that it did not intend to call the remaining 27 as the 11 called, plus the statements admitted by consent, were sufficient to establish a *prima facie* case. Subsequently, the Crown gave notice of a further 25 witnesses to be called at the trial. Thus, the defence was denied the opportunity to assess or cross-examine some 52 witnesses before the trial.

In sexual cases, the complainant's evidence is admitted by way of written statement unless leave is obtained from the court for the complainant to be called for cross-examination. As the complainant's evidence almost invariably of itself establishes a *prima facie* case, effectively there is no need for a deposition hearing at all in these cases. The prosecutor can simply hand up the complainant's statement which of itself establishes a *prima facie* case and a committal for trial must ensue without more.

Since the enactment of section 173A of the Summary Proceedings Act 1957 allowing evidence to be given by way of statement at depositions with the consent of the defendant, many depositions hearings are, as a matter of practice, conducted entirely upon the papers with no witnesses giving evidence *viva voce* at all. In a large number of cases, some witnesses give evidence *viva voce* and some by way of written statement, the choice being that of the defendant.

In its 1990 Report on *Criminal Procedure*[5] the Law Commission proposed that preliminary hearings be conducted on the basis that prosecution evidence be accepted in the form of a written statement unless personal attendance is required by the court of its own motion or on the application of any party, and that cross-examination of prosecution witnesses be by leave and only for 'limited recognisable practical reasons'. Leave would be granted only if:

a. the witness is to give evidence of identification of the defendant;
b. the witness is to give evidence of an alleged confession;
c. the witness is alleged to have been an accomplice in the crime; or
d. the witness has made an apparently inconsistent statement.

In June 1996 a proposal emanated from the Department of Courts proposing either the modification or the abolition of preliminary hearings with a preference being expressed for abolition. The legal profession in general seems to be of the view that this proposal is driven by fiscal reasons.

In its Preliminary Paper on *Criminal Prosecution* (1997) the Law Commission asked:[6]

Should preliminary hearings be retained if the Commission's proposals for reform are adopted? If so, in what form?

In the same Paper the Commission observed:[7]

Another principal function of the preliminary hearing in modern times has been to inform the defendant of the Crown's case. This has to some extent been achieved outside of the hearing by the inauguration of an effective criminal disclosure regime.

The Commission went on to note that in its 1990 Report it proposed a more sophisticated disclosure regime.

The proposition that effective disclosure obviates the need for a preliminary hearing necessarily involves acceptance that a legitimate and proper function of the preliminary hearing is to fully inform the defendant of the Crown's case. The author and many experienced defence counsel would assert that this is not only a legitimate and proper function of the preliminary hearing, but that it should be accorded legal recognition as a right enforceable by the defendant.

It is accepted that the primary function of the preliminary hearing is to establish whether there is a *prima facie* case, in order to prevent cases proceeding to trial which have no real prospect of success. The classic examples of no *prima facie* case are:

a. when there is no evidence whatsoever of an essential legal ingredient of the charge; and
b. when the evidence for the prosecution is so discredited,

whether by cross-examination or by other evidence, that no jury properly directed could safely act upon it.

The answer to the legal question of whether there is any evidence of each of the essential legal ingredients of the charge can be ascertained from an examination of the exhibits and the witness statements. The quality or creditability (as distinct from credibility) of the evidence cannot. That can only be ascertained by a hearing, and usually following cross-examination. The absence of creditability may also be established by other evidence of witnesses to be called by the prosecution and particularly as a result of cross-examination of those witnesses.

Frequently, defence counsel will require witnesses to give evidence *viva voce* at depositions and not cross-examine at all. There is a perfectly legitimate and proper forensic reason for doing so. Deposition statements are virtually always prepared by the police. Frequently, they are in the words of the police officer preparing them and contain what the prosecutor would like the witness to say. Whether the witness will say that when those words are not put in his or her mouth by the prosecutor may be a very different matter. It is a necessary part of trial preparation to satisfy oneself that prosecution witnesses will indeed give the evidence the prosecution proposes to lead. If they do not and, as a result, there is no evidence of an essential legal ingredient of the charge then there will be no *prima facie* case and a case doomed to failure will not proceed to trial.

For these reasons alone, the screening process which is the primary function of the preliminary hearing requires that the defence should have the right to require witnesses to appear and give evidence and be cross-examined.

Similarly, an essential part of trial preparation in the case of some witnesses may be simply to assess the witness in advance and/or explore whether the witness is able to give evidence under cross-examination which will assist the defence. Whilst it is true that defence counsel have the right to interview prosecution witnesses, both before and after the depositions hearing, it is equally true that witnesses are not obliged to be interviewed by the defence. Thus the right to interview may be of little utility.

It is submitted that the right to have witnesses give evidence *viva voce* at a preliminary hearing, and the right to cross-examine them, is encompassed in the right to adequate facilities to prepare a defence contained in section 24 (d) of the New Zealand Bill of Rights Act 1990.

Not infrequently Crown Prosecutors seek to supplement evidence given at depositions by providing notice of intention to call additional witnesses or evidence, often at a late stage. In *R* v *Bennett*[8] Tipping J stated:

It is becoming quite an epidemic in my experience and in the experience of other Judges of this Court that the Crown seeks to supplement material from the depositions frequently at the very last minute, sometimes leading to the abortion of trials. This is something which this Court does not view with favour.

In *R* v *Niania and Bridge*[9] Williamson J stated:

It is often said and perhaps should be repeated that trials of serious matters cannot involve trial by ambush. It is important that adequate notice be given to the person accused of a crime of the evidence which is available.

In that case, as in *Bennett*, the Court refused to allow the late evidence to be led. In other cases, despite lateness and judicial criticism of it, courts have allowed it to be led. At the present time there is no particular rule or principle other than the judge's assessment of the competing interests of the accused in a fair trial and the interests of society in securing the conviction of the guilty.

It is submitted that this state of affairs is unsatisfactory. The right to adequate time and facilities to prepare a defence and the right to a fair trial under the New Zealand Bill of Rights Act both encompass the right, not only to be fully informed well in advance of the case against an accused person, but also of the right to test the veracity of the witness and of the evidence before trial in crimes sufficiently serious to be proceeded against on indictment.

There have been no steps taken to implement the Law Commission's proposals for a more comprehensive regime of compulsory disclosure. The present regime is inconsistent, haphazard and unsatisfactory in practice. While this state of affairs continues, the argument that the advent of disclosure has removed or reduced the need for preliminary hearings lacks proper foundation.

IV Some Current Problems

1 The Jury System

There are two notable features of high profile, complex jury cases which have become common in recent years, namely:

a. very lengthy deliberations by the jury; and
b. inability of the jury to reach a unanimous verdict.

The law provides that if after four hours of consideration a jury has not reached a verdict, the judge may discharge the jury and order a new trial.[10] Twenty years ago it was virtually unheard of in New Zealand for a jury to deliberate on its verdict for more than a day. This was so even in cases involving multiple defendants — in an unlawful assembly trial against some 30 defendants in which the author was involved, which lasted three weeks, a jury was still able to reach verdicts on each defendant and on each charge within eight hours. In a case involving one defendant or two, six hours was considered a long time and anything more than that generally tended to be regarded as unsatisfactory, carrying a real risk of a compromise and not a true verdict being reached.

In the last few years it has become common for juries to deliberate for days. At the same time, there appears to be an increasing trend for juries to fail to agree. Notable examples in the last two years have been the cases of *R* v *Barlow*, the Thomas father and son shooting in downtown Wellington, where Barlow was eventually convicted of murder at the end of the third trial, two juries having failed to agree; and *R* v *Calder*, the 'Poisoned Professor' case in Christchurch, where the accused was alleged to have administered acrylamide to her former lover. This case resulted in an acquittal after the first jury were unable to agree. It is impossible to obtain empirical evidence as to the cause of these phenomena because of the sanctity which the law accords to the jury's deliberations, prohibiting the questioning of what occurs within the jury room. I suggest, however, that they are linked, there being factors common to each. I shall endeavour to explore these, but in no particular order of rank.

Expert evidence, whether of chemical analyses, DNA and other blood testing procedures, fingerprints, paper, handwriting, ballistics, pathology, computer processes, to name but a few, are increasingly common features of today's major complex trials. It has to be questioned whether a jury of 12 men and women drawn at random from the population can reasonably be expected to comprehend, let alone properly analyse and apply, the complexities of this kind of evidence. Defence counsel usually cannot do so without the assistance of their own experts. Why should we expect juries to be better equipped than defence counsel, especially when the experts cannot agree?

It is not uncommon for the police to adduce scientific evidence, in itself perfectly accurate, but which is used to advance an argument which the proved fact does not support. For instance, evidence is given that fragments of glass from the crime scene are of the same refractive index as glass connected to the accused. It is then argued that this conclusively links the accused with the crime scene, and is a strong item of circumstantial evidence. This is quite misleading. Without evidence of the percentage of glass in New Zealand having the same refractive index, and the uses to which such glass is commonly put and thus where it can be expected to be found, it is not capable of supporting any inference at all. In similar vein is evidence that paint found at the crime scene is of a similar colour and resin base to paint connected with the accused. Without more, this type of evidence provides no probative connection at all, and yet it is frequently presented and then used as the basis of argument to link the accused to the scene. Unless expert evidence is clearly presented and its logical significance, using accepted probability theory and statistical method, is properly explained by the experts — and not by counsel endeavouring to place some probative significance on it which it does not bear — the juries are likely to be at best confused and at worst misled.

Quite apart from the complexities of expert evidence is the sheer difficulty of assimilating, absorbing, collating and analysing the evidence of many witnesses — sometimes in the hundreds — over a period of weeks with no record other than the jurors' own handwritten notes taken in the jury box. Judges and counsel have the luxury of a reasonably full record taken by the Judge's Associate. In the days when the transcript was recorded on multiple copy carbon paper on a typewriter it was obviously impracticable to provide the jury with a transcript. Modern technology has overcome those practical limitations. Is there any valid reason why the persons charged with the duty of deciding the guilt or innocence of the accused should not have available to them a full record of the evidence upon which they are required to make that decision? Is the rationale behind the present practice that the full record is likely to distract the jury from making their decision based on broad assessments of the evidence and the witnesses, rather than a detailed comparison and analysis of the evidence — which may well take a very long time? If that is the case, then is that not in itself an argument that such cases are unsuitable for trial by jury?

The adequacy of the directions given to the jury may well be a contributing factor to uncertainties resulting in lengthy deliberations and disagreements. The present approved formula for a direction as to the meaning of 'a reasonable doubt' is along the lines of:

A reasonable doubt is exactly that, no more and no less. It is a doubt based on reason. It is not a vague and fanciful doubt conjured up out of the air to avoid an unpleasant duty. It is not beyond all doubt but it is beyond a reasonable doubt, i.e. a doubt which is based on reason.

With respect, it is submitted that this formulation creates

257

more confusion than clarity. It is essentially an ellipsis; a reasonable doubt is a reasonable doubt is a reasonable doubt.

Juries used to be directed that a reasonable doubt meant the kind of doubt which they would need to have satisfied themselves about before taking some serious step affecting their own lives. Whilst that kind of direction eventually succumbed to criticism that it failed to provide any objective standard, it did at least provide jurors with something which they could understand and relate to. Notably, in a high profile case in Auckland in 1997, after several hours of deliberation the jury returned with a question, namely, could the judge direct them on what constitutes a reasonable doubt. Given that the standard approved formula had already been provided, one has to wonder what, if anything, was achieved by its repetition in answer to that question.

If the best legal minds are unable to formulate a concise and simple explanation of the most fundamental concept in the criminal law which a jury of ordinary men and women can understand and apply, one has to seriously question whether the jury system is any longer relevant to modern society.

As we enter the 21st century I submit that we have to question whether the jury system, which had its origins in the days of Henry II, is really still appropriate, at least as presently constituted, as an instrument to decide complex cases. A very senior and experienced professional colleague has frequently stated that 'everyone should have the right *not* to be tried by a jury'.

The qualification 'as presently constituted' in the preceding paragraph needs further elucidation. There are those within the practising legal profession who believe that, because criminal trials of any length and complexity make considerable demands on the time of jurors, who are extremely poorly paid, and represent a considerable intrusion into their lives, many prospective jurors with the wit to do so find some basis on which to escape from service. This means that many jurors are those who have nothing better to do, and/or are quite prepared to spend days and weeks so engaged. That may be regarded as a harsh and unfair criticism, but nonetheless it is a view which is held and expressed. If it is true, then the quality of the mental processes of the jurors may not be adequate to the task they are asked to perform. I suggest that the right to a fair trial 'by an independent and impartial Court' conferred by section 25 (a) New Zealand Bill of Rights Act 1990 implies that the jury, as the decider of fact and the ultimate issue, must be capable of understanding and analysing the factual issues, as well as the legal directions as to the law it is to apply.

The spectre of an American style jury empanelling system, with questioning of jurors as part of the selection system, has cost implications which will be most unwelcome in the cost-conscious market-force ideology which dominates current political processes. However, if the jury system is to be retained into the 21st century then it is submitted that it must adapt to the nature of the environment in which it is required to function. That may well involve assessment of individual jurors as being not only impartial, but intellectually capable of assimilating and understanding the complex material which will be presented to them, and reaching a rational reasoned decision. The alternative is that justice is a lottery.

Appellate courts are extremely reluctant to disturb the verdicts of juries. The ground of appeal that the verdict is unreasonable or cannot be supported by the evidence (section 385(1)(a) Crimes Act 1961) is the most difficult of all on which to succeed on appeal. This judicial reluctance to interfere must be based on the premise that the courts can have confidence in the decisions of juries. That confidence must be, and be shown to be, justified and justifiable. It is submitted that there is at least some reasonable doubt on that issue.

2 Inequality of Resources

In any criminal trial, but especially in major and complex cases of serious crime, the police have enormous resources at their disposal. Unless the accused is enormously wealthy he or she cannot hope to match those resources without the assistance of the state.

Article 14 (1) of the International Covenant on Human Rights requires that 'all persons shall be equal before the Court and Tribunals'. In Continental European jurisprudence this statement is given expression in the concept of 'Equality of Arms'. The doctrine has been referred to in a number of cases in New Zealand, both in the High Court and the Court of Appeal. In particular, in *R* v *B*[11] Hardie Boys J in the Court of Appeal described it as a 'well recognised principle ... which finds expression in the Bill of Rights provisions.' It was considered further again by a court of five judges of the Court of Appeal in *Wellington District Law Society* v *Tangiora*,[12] in *R* v *Brown*[13] and again in *R* v *Barlow*,[14] with apparent acceptance that the doctrine applies as part of New Zealand law.

In *R* v *Brown*[15] the relevant District Legal Services Committee had declined an application by defence counsel to have DNA testing carried out in Sydney. The exhibit in question had already been examined by the ESR in New Zealand but for a different purpose and the ESR itself considered that it was not able to carry out the testing itself. It was submitted there was a breach of the principle of Equality of Arms resulting in a breach of section 24

(d) of the New Zealand Bill of Rights Act (adequate time and facilities to prepare a defence), and also breach of the rights under section 25 (the right to a fair hearing, the right to present a defence and 'to obtain the attendance and examination of witnesses for the defence under the same conditions as the Prosecution'). The Criminal Appeal Division of the Court of Appeal referred the argument to the Permanent Bench of the Court of Appeal for consideration. However, as a result of a further DNA test carried out by ESR the argument was not pursued, as the appeal was allowed and a new trial ordered as a result of new evidence obtained from that test.

Many defence counsel have similar experiences of funding or full funding for scientific examination being refused by the Legal Aid authorities. Likewise, defence counsel are often under severe financial constraints in respects of their own time, preparation and research. *Prima facie* these financial restraints are breaches of the Equality of Arms principle and the provisions of the New Zealand Bill of Rights Act which give expression to that principle. So long as these breaches continue there will continue to be, at the very least, a perception of unfairness in the criminal investigation and trial process. This is exacerbated and compounded by the short-comings in the present disclosure regime and, in particular, by instances of deliberate suppression of unfavourable evidence by the prosecution.

3 *Control and Accountability of the Investigative Process*

The New Zealand Police are not subject to any form of political control. The police force is a hierarchical structure organised on paramilitary lines. Regulations require each member to obey the applicable regional and district orders and the lawful commands of a superior. The police must also comply with police general instructions and circulars issued by the highest ranking officer, the Commissioner of Police.[16]

Actions of the police which the courts consider to be an abuse of process, or breach of an accused person's rights under the New Zealand Bill of Rights Act, may result in the courts exercising their inherent powers to control their own process by refusing to admit evidence or, in rare cases, ordering a stay of proceedings. However, the courts have no control over the actions of police officers except, of course, where criminal offences have been committed and the officers have been brought before the court to answer the charges.

In effect, therefore, the police are only accountable to themselves. In the introduction to this paper reference was made to the futility of complaints to the police about the actions of police officers. No doubt as a response to growing public concern about lack of accountability, the Police Complaints Authority Act was enacted in 1988, providing for the appointment of an independent authority with inquisitorial powers and powers of recommendation. Under the Act the Authority may investigate any complaint made to the police and referred to it by the police, or may investigate any complaint made to it independently, or may carry out a joint enquiry in conjunction with the police.

However the Authority does not employ its own investigators independently of the police. All investigation work is carried out on behalf of the Authority by police officers. Not infrequently, the complaint is investigated by officers from the same district and even the same station as the officer or officers against whom the complaint is made. There is widespread dissatisfaction with this process both by persons making complaints and by lawyers acting for them.

It needs to be said that there are many policemen throughout the country who are of the highest moral integrity and trust-worthiness. However, I doubt that there is one defence lawyer in the country who at some time or another has not had experience of the kinds of malpractice referred to in this paper. Former police officers, from one end of the country to the other, have confirmed that not only do practices such as suppression of evidence and, indeed, its tailoring to fit the charge go on, but these are an accepted and expected part of the police culture. Officers are expected to be loyal to other officers in the sense that they will cover up for them and for the organisation. I have spoken to former officers who informed me that they left the force because their personal integrity would not allow them to co-operate in or condone such practices. Often, it is not until they are free of the pressures to conform to the organisational ethic that the police are and must be seen to be infallible, that they see this for what it is.

It is hardly surprising therefore that in carrying out investi-gations of complaints, that organisational ethic dominates. My own experience, and that of many other lawyers with whom I have discussed the matter, and of the complainants themselves, is that the investigation is used as a means to exonerate the officer or officers involved, and to absolve the Police Force in general from any blame or criticism. Even where serious short-comings in the course of an investigation are clearly identified, these are found to be excusable. Responses to the effect that defence counsel should have exposed the truth, that the officer didn't think it important or necessary or his responsibility to correct a misleading impression, pressure of work, the officer can't remember doing/saying the subject matter of the complaint, the transcript or other record is wrong, the facts are different to those stated on oath to be the case, and the complainant was guilty anyway, appear to be accepted as excusing whatever occurred.

In the rare case in which severe criticism is made, the Authority has no power to discipline the officers concerned. That remains a matter within the discretion of the police hierarchy. Internal police disciplinary procedures may be invoked, and if so (as far as one can gather because the proceedings are *in camera*) the outcome is usually that the offending officers receive counselling.

An example of the organisational ethic and attitude described is to be seen in events following the recent report from the Police Complaints Authority regarding the Wicked Willies Night Club case in Christchurch referred to earlier in this paper. Notwith-standing the Authority's comments in the published report that the police officer's actions (destroying and not disclosing to the defence a statement clearly identifying another person as the offender and exonerating the accused) were quite incredible, the Regional Commander of the Police District announced publicly that the Police would be making no apologies to the man wrongly arrested and charged with murder!

Even where proved to be wrong, the police steadfastly refuse to admit it. This philosophy of protecting the police from criticism, even where it is deserved, ensures not only that corrupt practices in the investigative process and the prosecution process will continue unless radical reforms are introduced, but that there can be no confidence in the present system so long as the police continue to investigate the police. Police Complaints Authority investigations must be carried out by persons entirely separate from and independent of the police.

Proposals for Reform

1 The Law Commission's Proposals

The Law Commission's 1997 Preliminary Paper on *Criminal Prosecution* expressly excludes from its ambit the investigative process. It does make the point that 'It is essential for investigative and prosecution decisions to be made more distinct and independent',[17] but concludes that this can be achieved by building on and improving the present system.

The Commission makes a number of proposals for reform of the prosecution process including proposals to increase control and accountability, proposals regarding charge negotiation, prosecutor's powers, and the structure of the prosecution system, including the separation of investigation and prosecution functions. In particular, it cites the 1981 Report of the UK Royal Commission on Criminal Procedure for the proposition that:

A police officer who carries out an investigation inevitably and properly forms a view as to the guilt of the subject. Having done so, without any kind of improper motive, that officer may be inclined to shut his or her mind to other evidence telling against the guilt of the suspect and to overestimate the strength of the evidence . . . assembled.

The Law Commission recommends that prosecution decisions should be made by a person detached from the investigation process.

The Commission's preferred option, however, is not for there to be an independent Crown Prosecution Service (apparently because of 'significant resource costs that would accompany' such a service) but favours Crown Solicitors becoming independent public prosecutors who would become involved in a prosecution as soon as indictable information has been filed in the court or the defendant has elected trial by jury. The Paper notes that 'mechanisms for control over prosecutions and public accountability of prosecutors are few.'[18] In respect of summary (i.e. non-indictable) prosecutions, the Commission recommends the establishment of 'an autonomous and career-orientated national police prosecution service, . . . administratively distinct from the criminal investigation and uniform branches of the police.'[19]

2 A Different View

I suggest that the unsatisfactory aspects of the present systems of investigation and prosecution may be derived from the fundamental nature of the present common law system — i.e. its adversarial nature. The very nature of the adversary system promotes the concept that the investigation and prosecution of crime is a contest between opposing sides in which, in order to succeed, it is necessary to present only one side of the case and hinder the presentation of the other side to the greatest extent possible in the context of this contest. The object of the exercise is to succeed and thereby defeat the other player in the game.

The competitive element underlying the system promotes and justifies the tactics of reluctance to disclose one's hand, to deliberately or inadvertently suppress important evidence, or to present facts in an incomplete and misleading manner. This in fact happens, and it happens because it is in the nature of the human being to strive to win. When winning is perceived to be of social utility, by bringing offenders to justice, the temptation to cheat is significant. The end is seen as justifying the means. As the UK Royal Commission on Criminal Procedure pointed out in the passage cited above, the shutting of the mind of the police officer may be inadvertent. However inadvertence is no excuse for a miscarriage of justice.

The British author Ludovic Kennedy, at the New Zealand Law Society Triennial Conference held in Christchurch in 1980, argued that many of the miscarriages of justice in notorious cases are a direct result of the excesses and failings of the adversary system, and that the inquisitorial system of European continental jurisprudence, where the investigation is conducted under the control of a judicial officer (*juge d'instruction*) is better designed and better able to achieve not only truth but justice. Some of the more notorious examples of police malpractice which have emerged in the United Kingdom since then — e.g. the cases of the 'Guildford Four' and the 'Birmingham Six' — have added strength to his arguments.

It is salutary to remember that the police began as a peace-keeping organisation in the early 19th century and gradually acquired the roles of investigator and prosecutor by default, being drawn into the vacuum created by the decline of the investigatory role of the grand jury. There is no statutory authority conferring either role on the police.

The position of Crown Solicitor developed in the mid-19th century in New Zealand as a result of the needs of the colony at that time. There is criticism within the practising profession that many Crown Solicitors today are too close to the police, and lack the independence and objectivity that the role requires. The competitive basis of the adversary system must influence both the perception and the reality.

The lack of fairness, consistency, transparency and account-ability of the investigative process have resulted in defence lawyers today having to assume the dual role of counter-investigator as well as advocate for the defence. Increasing use of private investigators — often ex-police personnel — is being

267

made by defence counsel. Sadly, this is becoming a necessity because of the lack of confidence engendered by the excesses of the present system. Such independent investigation does on a number of occasions lead to charges being withdrawn. Thus the roles are blurred even further. A system of open investigation in which the public and the profession can be confident of its independence, objectivity and integrity would allow counsel to return to their proper role as advocates, reduce duplication of effort and resources and hence improve efficiency, and promote the proper objectives of truth and justice.

The Law Commission's proposals are based on the premise that the present system can be effectively improved, although it does suggest the need to consider 'more radical reform' if necessary improvement does not occur.[20] With respect to the Commission's impressive analysis and research, I suggest that its proposals address the outward effects of the problem, and not the underlying cause. The root cause, it is suggested, is the adversarial system itself and the resulting concept of a contest between opposing sides in which only one will emerge as the winner. The result of this is that truth, justice and fairness frequently emerge as the losers — whether the immediate result be conviction or acquittal.

There is room to question whether the present system is in fact wholly adversarial. It is open to argument that inquisitorial elements are allowed to intrude where that is seen to favour the interests of the state. I refer in particular to the current practice of allowing one or even two re-trials where a jury cannot agree: *R* v *Barlow* is a particular example. In a purely adversarial system, is there any justification to allow the Crown a replay simply because it has failed to win the first game? Does the right of the accused to a fair trial have to be read as subject to the right of the

Crown to try again, often as in *Barlow* with additional evidence to plug the holes exposed in the first trial, because it was unable to get it right the first time? Or is the hidden premise an acceptance that juries are incompetent or irrational to an extent which it is not expedient to admit?

It is now time, I suggest, to openly consider and debate the basic philosophy and structures of the present system, and the justification for their continued existence, or abandonment, or their replacement by a coherent and unified system suited to today's society. I submit that the first question to be asked is whether a system and philosophy which has developed in an *ad hoc* manner over many centuries is an appropriate basis for the administration of the criminal justice system in the new millennium. Only when that question has been answered should the detail be addressed.

Footnotes

1 [1975] 2 NZLR 289.
2 [1988] 1 NZLR 385.
3 See Law Commission, *Compensation for Wrongful Conviction or Prosecution*, Preliminary Paper No 31, April 1998.
4 High Court, Invercargill, October 1995.
5 Law Commission, Report No 14, *Criminal Procedure — Part I — Disclosure and Committal* (1990).
6 Law Commission, *Criminal Prosecution*, Preliminary Paper No 28, 1997, p18, Q43.
7 Ibid at para 449.
8 High Court, Timaru, T12/90, 11 October 1990.
9 High Court, Invercargill, T16/88, 23 May 1989.
10 Crimes Act 1961, s374(2).
11 [1995] 2 NZLR 172, 184.
12 CA 33/97, 10 September 1997.
13 CA 32/96, 29 July 1996.
14 CA 581/95, 21 August 1995.
15 Supra n 13.
16 See Police Regulations 1992, SR 192/14.

17 Supra n 6 at par 342.
18 Ibid at p59.
19 Ibid at para 353.
20 Ibid at para 345.

Appendix II

Is it time to reform an unjust legal system?

The following is taken from an address by Peter Williams QC to the Criminal Bar Association in Auckland in 1999. Continued miscarriages of justice, he says, suggest that the search for truth should play a greater role in our justice system.

There has always been a conflict in our courts between seeking justice and following the letter of the law.

We are practising law in an era where the judicial emphasis is on the pedantic letter of the law rather than justice in the broad sense.

There is a danger that our lawyers and judges have already developed a legalistic ivory tower that is remote from the reality of everyday living.

This highly studied approach to problems relies upon precedent and formalised procedures, making the court process so complex and artificial that only lawyers or, indeed, highly sophisticated lawyers, know how to operate its refined machinery.

Already the public is sceptical about our courts, lawyers and judges. Its perception is that this unfathomable forensic domain has been established by the legal profession for its own benefit, and the mystique has been artificially created to keep out laypeople, thereby establishing a lucrative monopoly for itself.

It may well be that in the past there has been a pecuniary benefit to the legal profession in keeping a tightly closed shop in this way. But our social system has developed over the years and become more democratic and transparent and the public is now intolerant of judicial conceit, pomposity and arrogance. Examples of this extravagant behaviour have been personified in the past, particularly by some of the senior judges of England.

Ordinary citizens now require our judicial system to be accountable and pragmatic. An example is people's attitude towards legal aid. Because laypeople generally regard our court advocates with suspicion, there is reluctance to accept that money appropriated from the taxpayer to fund this essential service is well spent.

Advocates, by the very nature of the criminal justice adversary system, do not necessarily pursue the truth, but instead develop arguments that will win the case for their clients. Successful lawyers must be Machiavellian and devious. If a particular lawyer is invariably honest and open, his fellow practitioners regard him as being naive.

Let us compare this wily professional aspiration of the trial lawyer with other professions. Medical practitioners honestly apply their skills and knowledge to healing the maladies of their patients. Civil engineers worth their salt apply their wisdom and training in designing bridges and buildings that will be durable and reliable. I know of no other vocation where the qualified expert is not expected to encourage truth and essential soundness in the fruits of his or her labour.

From the ranks of the trial lawyers, the trickiest and most formidable are sometimes chosen to be judges. It is not surprising that judges may be prickly and awkward and, instead of consistently seeking the truth, craft their judgments upon precedents and legal fictions to avoid the humiliation of being upset on appeal.

There is a real danger that the procedures in our courts have become the equivalent of a complex and dangerous game where advocates are expected to know the intricacies and subtle rules, and learn to manipulate these difficult concepts to the advantage of their paying customers.

The issue is whether the time has arrived when we should seriously consider simplifying the procedures in our criminal courts and abate unnecessary legalese and hoi polloi clogging up and unnecessarily obstructing the true process of justice.

Should we consider abolishing the adversary system completely and adopting a new system based on the European inquisitorial system? In France, when the paparazzi were unjustifiably accused of responsibility for the death of Princess Diana, this system seemed to work efficiently.

The large number of miscarriages of justice in serious criminal cases that have continued to occur in both New Zealand and British courts over the past few years indicate that all is not well in our legal machine.

Reforms that go right to the fundamentals of our procedures are urgently needed. These would incorporate a greater search for the truth and allow more realism into the criminal legal process.

Again and again, the innocence of a wrongly convicted person has only been exposed by the work of journalists and laypeople.

Appendix III

Chronology

1996

JANUARY   I read a *New Zealand Herald* article about the Friends of David Bain, contact David Bain's lawyer and meet David.

FEBRUARY/MARCH/APRIL

I make an intensive study of the police files and trial transcript supplied to me by Michael Guest, David's defence counsel.

29 APRIL   David Bain's appeal to the Privy Council fails.

JUNE   I meet frequently with David Bain, and meet with the police in Dunedin. I dismiss Michael Guest, and appoint Stephen O'Driscoll and Colin Withnall QC to assist me. I meet Dean Cottle and other witnesses.

JULY   An appeal by the *Holmes* programme leads to the suppression order on Dean Cottle's name and evidence being overturned.

AUGUST/SEPTEMBER

I continue to investigate the case. The *20/20* documentary on the case is screened.

OCTOBER   I meet with the Commissioner of Police, Peter
                 Doone.

NOVEMBER   I decide to write a book.

1997

JANUARY   I write *David and Goliath*. Colin Withnall QC
                 makes a public statement that in his opinion
                 David has suffered a miscarriage of justice.

16 APRIL   *David and Goliath* is published.

MAY   A joint police/Police Complaints Authority (PCA)
                 review into 'unfounded allegations' against the
                 police in *David and Goliath* is announced.

JUNE   *Mask of Sanity*, by James McNeish, is published.
                 Wicked Willies nightclub calls me.
                 John Joseph calls me.

JULY   I meet with the police/PCA review team.

AUGUST   I obtain a number of exhibits in the Bain case
                 for examination at forensic laboratories in
                 Melbourne.

26 NOVEMBER   The report of the police/PCA review is released.

DECEMBER   I study the police/PCA report.

1998

JANUARY   I obtain source documents in relation to the
                 police/PCA review, including ESR (Environ-
                 mental Science and Research) reports. I visit the

ESR in Auckland, and obtain 'fingerprint' blood sample for independent analysis.

FEBRUARY   I obtain the 'luminol photographs', whose existence has previously been denied.

MARCH   The PCA reopens the file on the key Bain witness Denise Laney, and other issues relating to disclosure of evidence.

APRIL   Detective Sergeant Milton Weir and Detective Sergeant Kevin Anderson initiate defamation proceedings against me, claiming damages totalling over $500,000.

MAY   Arie Geursen obtains a DNA result on the fingerprint blood on David Bain's rifle.

16 JUNE   Four years after David Bain's arrest, a petition is filed with the Governor-General seeking a royal pardon.

BALANCE OF 1998

           Correspondence and meetings with Ministry of Justice officials on petition issues.

1999

JANUARY   Meetings with Ministry of Justice officials, ESR and Arie Geursen.

FEBRUARY/MARCH

           Receive police and Crown Law Office responses to David's petition.

JULY	I meet with Ministry of Justice officials in Wellington to finalise petition issues. They advise that the report should be complete in two to three months at the latest.
NOVEMBER	Change of government; new Minister of Justice, Phil Goff.
DECEMBER	Ministry of Justice now advises that its report is being sent to a QC for independent peer review.

2000

MARCH	Begin writing *Bain and Beyond*.
APRIL	Ministry of Justice advises that its report is instead being sent to a retired High Court judge for peer review.
29 MAY	The defamation case against me begins in the High Court in Auckland.
9 JUNE	The defamation case ends, with the jury finding in my favour on all claims.
JULY	Preparation of further submissions to the Ministry of Justice as a result of the evidence in the defamation trial.